Love Yourself

The First Step to a Successful Relationship

Daniel Beaver, M.S. M.F.T.

cognella™

San Diego, CA

First published in the United States of America in 2010 by Cognella, a division of University Readers, Inc.

Trademark Notice: Product or corporate names may be trademarks or registered trademarks, and are used only for identification and explanation without intent to infringe.

15 14 13 12 11 1 2 3 4 5

Printed in the United States of America

ISBN: 978-1-60927-830-4

www.cognella.com 800.200.3908

CONTENTS

This book is dedicated to my loving and supportive wife, Nancy, who has given me the gift of what it's like to be loved for who I am.

And to my two loving daughters, Danielle and Michelle. Please love yourselves; you both are wonderful women.

INTRODUCTION

*L*ove *Yourself* is my third published book dealing with the subject of intimacy. It completes my trilogy of books dealing with the subject of intimacy that has evolved over thirty-five years of being a therapist and college professor in the area of relationships and personal growth. In hindsight, it's clear to me that loving yourself and having positive self-esteem is key to developing a healthy, long-lasting relationship. Loving yourself lays the fundamental psychological foundation on which a relationship can be built. It's hard to look at yourself first and do the work that it takes to love yourself. I hope in reading this book that you will find it easier to love yourself and find a clearer path to fulfillment.

It seems odd that people have to learn how to love themselves, but in this culture, it's a challenge. Like all the areas of intimacy, whether emotional or sexual, we need information on how to accomplish the goal of self-love. There is nothing natural about self-love; it requires learning and unlearning attitudes and behaviors that undermine the goal of self-love.

As with my other two books, *Creating the Intimate Connection* and *More Than Just Sex,* I examine the rather vague concept of loving yourself and take the subject to a very pragmatic and down-to-earth level. I want the reader to apply the material in this book to their life and make some positive changes in the areas of self-love and self-esteem. I provide real-life examples so that you can learn from my experience and from all the patients and students who have shared their experiences with me. I was truly someone who didn't love myself and was able to make the transformation to self-love. I hope the material in this book will give you the tools to make the same personal changes.

Be prepared to give up what you think is right or wrong, and open yourself up to what works. In the psychological world of attitude and behavioral change, it's about effecting changes in your life. It's not about arguing or debating how your life should be, but instead what works for you in achieving the goal of loving yourself. When a person moves out of their comfort zone, they are stepping into a whole new world, and there is a tendency to hang on to the old, even though it's causing psychological difficulty. Taking the risk to love yourself may be scary and awkward at first, but after a while, your new attitudes and behaviors will become the norm, and I am sure that your life will be enriched.

Any names or cases used as examples in this book have been changed for reasons of confidentiality. Any similarity to real-life situations is coincidental.

Lastly, I want to give a special thanks to Rosemary Gretton for all her editorial support in the writing of this book.

Chapter One

The Cognitive Behavioral Approach

I am often asked whether a person can really change who they are after so many years of living. Can you really teach an old dog new tricks? Can you really learn to love yourself and develop positive self-esteem and self-confidence? The answer to all of these questions is yes. If an individual is motivated to change and is open to developing new attitudes and beliefs, then it is possible. Over the years of practicing psychotherapy, I have helped many of my patients and the students in my college and university classes bring about personal changes in their attitudes and behaviors.

The psychological approach I use in helping them make these changes is called cognitive-behavioral. I was introduced for the first time to this style of psychotherapy and teaching when I trained as a sex therapist. It was used as a treatment approach that had very good outcomes in a fairly short period. Eventually I began to use the cognitive behavioral approach in all my work with people. It didn't become a popular approach among therapists until managed mental health care took over the practice of psychotherapy in the United States. However, when health insurance companies saw that quick results could be achieved relatively quickly, they realized this approach was cost effective when compared to other styles of therapy.

A good understanding of this approach is a helpful starting point in the process of learning to love yourself. The word *cognitive* means the process of acquiring knowledge by use of reasoning, intuition, or perception. Cognitive refers to the attitudes, beliefs, and values that we have learned from our particular culture. These include both the overt and covert messages we receive from our families of origin, our educational experience, our religious training, our peer culture, and the all-encompassing media. We were taught how to think about how to be a man or a woman, wife or husband. We were taught what being successful meant or what being beautiful or sexy was all about. We were taught how to love ourselves or not. The majority of this teaching went on without our conscious knowledge, making it difficult to reject any of the beliefs. The messages that were overt and direct were delivered by authority figures, so we couldn't really question whether what they were saying made any sense. It's just the way it was. As a result, these messages were embedded into our everyday thinking, greatly influencing our personal lives, both positively and negatively.

The behavioral part of this approach relates to the actions we take in our everyday world--what we do in terms of interacting with other people in our business dealings or in our personal lives. It's the way we communicate with others and ourselves, the way we treat others and ourselves, and the way we make love. In this approach, most of our behavior stems from our cognitive thinking. Behavior is also learned from what we see in our families through the modeling process. It isn't so much what our parents said that we remember, but how they acted. These memories stick with us well into adult life. Similar to our cognitive beliefs, some of these behaviors are there without our knowing of their existence on a conscious level. They just come out of what seems like nowhere and suddenly we find ourselves acting like one of our parents. This could be a good thing, but it could also be a negative experience, depending on your point of view.

An example of this happened to me once when I was having dinner at a restaurant with my two daughters when they were teenagers. They ordered their food, and when it came, they didn't eat much. I got upset, and out of nowhere came the voice of my father, "If you two ordered all this food, then you have to finish what is on your plate." After I realized what I had said, I told them not to worry about it and recanted my earlier statement by telling them to eat what they could, but if they were full they needed to stop and we would take the rest home in a doggie bag. I heard my father's message about wasting food and money, but there was no concern about obesity. This is an example of how you can change a cognitive belief of the past and replace it with one of your own, which in turn changes your behavior.

Some therapists think if you change a patient's cognitive beliefs, their behavior will change as well. Others think that if the patient changes their behavior, their attitudes will change as well. I think it's best to take a two-pronged approach: helping patients change both cognitive beliefs as well as their behavior. Learning new beliefs and attitudes is great, but if that's where the learning stops, then it has just been an intellectual exercise. The challenge is putting the new thinking into action and integrating these beliefs into the behavior of everyday life. It requires mindfulness and motivation.

The reason that the cognitive-behavioral method works so well in helping people learn to love themselves and others is that both attitudes and behavior are learned. They are not genetic, meaning that you can't change them because they are biological givens. On the other hand, what is learned can change. With new information, we can replace the old beliefs; and if there wasn't an attitude to begin with, we can establish a new one. New behaviors can also be learned when we are given direction on how to act in new, more effective ways. I am learning new ways to hit a tennis ball every time I have a tennis lesson. It amazes me that I can still learn new techniques even after playing for 30 years. This same concept is true of our personal life.

Another important fact about the ability to change attitudes and behaviors is that it is possible regardless of gender. It is a common myth that an individual's sexual identity as a woman or a man somehow limits her or his ability to make changes. We are all taught the gender behavior and roles appropriate for our culture, but the keyword is *taught* and therefore we can make a change. In his book, *Men Are from Mars and Women Are from Venus*, John Gray reinforced the idea that we are stuck in these rigid gender roles, and that's just the way it is. Indeed, we are socialized a certain way, but that doesn't mean we can't change if we are given the information to make the change. I teach men in my psychotherapy practice how to be empathic and emotionally supportive. Once they know how to develop these behavioral traits and let go of the attitude that they have to fix their lovers' problems, changes can occur. I also teach women who traditionally act in a passive manner in their personal lives to become assertive behaviorally. I help them change their belief that being "nice" or passive is a positive behavior in an intimate relationship, and to see that in reality it is manipulative and doesn't foster self-love.

The other myth about cognitive and behavioral change is that once an individual reaches a certain age, they are unable to make changes in their personal life. Nothing could be further from the truth in my experience. I have helped people make changes in their personal lives regardless of age, as long as they were motivated and had the knowledge to make the change.

THE THREE KEYS FOR PERSONAL CHANGE

The first key component in order for personal change to occur is **conscious awareness:** the initial awareness that change needs to happen and then gaining the knowledge of how to change. Many people are unaware that they need to make changes in the way they may think or behave. Unfortunately, something often has to happen to them to come to this realization—some type of experience that produces consequences that challenge their current beliefs and behaviors. As in substance abuse recovery, they need to "hit bottom." The individual gets to a certain point emotionally or physically where they become motivated to change, not only from an intellectual understanding, but from an emotional one as well. The "wake-up call" occurs and the individual gains awareness about himself and the situation that gives him the insight that change is required.

The second key component that needs to be present for personal change to occur is **motivation**. Without motivation, personal change won't generally occur. Motivation is the spark or fuel that makes change happen. After I give a seminar and then open the discussion to questions, I often get what I call "how to get" questions, which sound like this: "How do I get my husband to share his feelings with me?" "How do I get my wife to stop drinking so much?" "How do I get my husband to go to marriage counseling?" "How do I get my husband to be more interested in having sex with me?" There are many more of these types of questions, but I hope you get the idea.

My answer to these questions is that you can't get someone to do anything unless you use force or manipulation, which I wouldn't recommend unless it's a life-or-death situation. You can't get another adult to change because you don't want control over an adult. It is different with children. If adults perceive that they are being controlled in some manner, they will resist the attempt to change and will feel a great deal of resentment as a result. This resentment will come back at whoever is trying to change them. I understand that these questions have a caring intent behind them, but that caring will be overshadowed because of the attempted control.

When I tell people who ask this type of question that they can't get this person to change, they often get upset to some degree. They want me to give them the professional advice that will give them the tools to "fix their partner." When I tell them they don't have that power, and that they don't even want that kind of control, they sometimes get upset because they have to confront the fact that they are powerless when it comes to trying to change someone else. We are all vulnerable, and that can be a hard concept to accept, especially when it relates to someone we care for deeply.

I remember all so clearly when my mother was dying of brain cancer, and I kept saying to the doctor: "So what are you going to do to take care of the malignant tumor growing in my mother's brain? Are you going to do surgery? Are you going to give her aggressive chemotherapy? Or are you going to do both?" His answer to all my questions was "No, there is nothing we can do for your mother; the situation is terminal." I replied, "What do you mean there is nothing you can do? There must be something." He repeated that there was nothing they could do for my mother. I was so angry with the doctor and the situation; but I was really angry that there was nothing I could do—I was powerless. I was vulnerable to the situation and had to accept that my mother's death was inevitable.

When people ask "how to get someone to change" questions, I respond by explaining that there is one thing they can do: **provide consequences** to whatever behavior they would like to see changed. I often come across the situation where a wife communicates her unhappiness with her husband's behavior, but when he doesn't change, she continues to go on as if everything is resolved when it's not. This is the classic double-message scenario where the behavior discounts the verbal message. The wife's walk doesn't match her talk. In other words, the husband has no consequences for continuing his behavior. There are many real-life examples of this pattern, and it can occur in all types of relationships, for instance, where the spouse's partner drinks too much, but keeps acting like it's not a problem the next day.

If the spouse expects no consequences, the behavior just keeps occurring. So what kinds of consequences might work? It depends on the situation and the person involved. The key that I find that motivates people to change their beliefs or behavior is emotion. Do they hurt enough, are they angry enough, or are they scared enough? What is enough emotion depends on the person. Emotions are great motivators for change. Another emotion that motivates people to change is pleasure. Usually, however, it's what people call the negative emotions that bring about change. Some type of experience has to happen where the emotional reaction is such that it motivates the individual to make a change.

In practice, I find that giving someone all kinds of reasons that make logical sense doesn't really work at bringing about change. The recipient of the information may listen and may even agree with you, but they don't change their behavior. This can be a very frustrating experience for the deliverer of the messages. You can point out example upon example to support your point of view, or build a great case of evidence that a person needs to change their behavior, but again this doesn't seem to go anywhere in trying to bring about change, because there are no emotional consequences.

Sometimes people react to the notion of giving someone an ultimatum as if this is a bad thing. If you drive intoxicated, the possible consequence is that you will be taken to jail and citied with a DUI. That's just the way it is in adult life. If consequences are taken away, then the motivation for change has also been removed. Not providing consequences or preventing a person from experiencing consequences is generally referred to as enabling.

The last component required for cognitive-behavioral change is the presence of **acceptance**. Without an atmosphere of acceptance, people tend to resist change. When they experience judgment or criticism, they avoid the person or the experience one way or another. They hold on even tighter to their behavior or belief. They may become defensive and stop listening. When the judgment or criticism is self-inflicted, an individual's motivation to change is undermined even if that isn't their intention.

Acceptance doesn't mean that you have to approve or like an individual's behavior or your own. What it does mean is that you don't assault your beliefs or behavior. It means that you don't attack your self-esteem or self-confidence. When acceptance exists, anger usually isn't present. What is present is self-love. Acceptance is a key component of loving yourself or another person. I will explore this in further detail in chapter seven.

THE THREE INTIMACIES

When I first started my career, my special focus was on the subject of sexual intimacy. I trained to become a sex therapist. After practicing sex therapy for a while, it became very clear to me that couples need to have a good foundation of emotional intimacy in order to have a fulfilling sex life. At that time, I wrote my first book, *Beyond the Marriage Fantasy*, which deals with the topic of emotional intimacy. Later in my career, it became clear to me that that self-love or intimacy with yourself has to exist in order to create emotional intimacy in a committed relationship.

Looking back, perhaps my professional development should have developed in the opposite direction: first self-intimacy, then emotional intimacy, and then sexual intimacy. I always teach the three intimacies in that order because developmentally that's what is more effective ideally. In reality, though, we don't learn these intimacies in such an orderly fashion.

Let's define the three intimacies.

Self-intimacy means that people are conscious of their internal emotional experience as it relates to what is occurring in their life. Once they have the awareness of their internal emotional experience, they can communicate these emotions externally. Self-intimacy occurs when people are honest, congruent, authentic, and in harmony with what they are feeling emotionally. This type of intimacy is the critical first step in achieving an emotionally intimate relationship. When people are involved in alcohol abuse or using drugs such as marijuana or cocaine, they become impaired in their ability to develop self-intimacy because these substances cut off their ability to experience true emotions. This is also true with people who are involved in other addictive behaviors such as working excessively or gambling or suffering from an eating disorder. These behaviors keep people from experiencing their true emotions, which again cripples them from having an intimate relationship with themselves and a significant other.

Emotional intimacy is generally created between two people who are in a committed relationship. Usually a great deal of trust exists between them, which allows them to be vulnerable and share and communicate their emotions with each other. Emotional intimacy is created and then lost in long-term relationships. The problem in Western culture is that when we lose the emotional intimacy, we don't have the behaviors or attitudes that allow us to recreate the intimacy. The assumption is that emotional intimacy should somehow just happen, and that we don't need to take a course or read a book to achieve it. When a couple starts to drift and they begin to lose the intimacy, they are constant struggling to recreate the emotional intimacy they once experienced in the beginning of their relationship. Many give up, not having the necessary tools or the skill set, and they begin to focus on other priorities such as raising children, developing a business career, or concentrating on some type of hobby or sports activity.

The third type of intimacy is **sexual intimacy**. This is the type of intimacy that most people think of when the word is used in common language. Sexual intimacy is the combination of where emotional intimacy exists and the couple is involved in a sexual experience. Without emotional intimacy being present, the couple is just having sex as opposed to "making love." This is what occurs in so many marriages today once they lose emotional intimacy. It is hard to go from acting like roommates outside the bedroom, and then turn around and go into the bedroom and have a passionate, intimate sexual experience. My second book, *More than Just Sex,* addressed these issues.

The primary focus of this book is how to maintain and create self-intimacy, which will lay the foundation for the development of emotional and sexual intimacy.

Chapter Two

Learning to Love Yourself

**"But if nobody loves you
and you feel like dust
on an empty shelve
just remember
you can love yourself"** —Keb Moe

When I first heard the phrase "learning to love yourself," it sounded like psychobabble. This saying is so vague. If I ask a client, "How do you love yourself?" I usually get a response that is just as vague. I intend to take this concept and make it very clear how to love yourself on both a cognitive and behavioral level. Just as I teach couples how to create emotional intimacy, I have the same goal of teaching individuals self-intimacy.

Does loving yourself mean saying, "Dan, I love you, you are so great." Not really, it's not that simple. Loving yourself in this context doesn't necessarily refer to masturbation, although that can be a part of the experience. The first major cognitive concept in learning to love yourself is that you need to respect and validate your own emotions. Whatever you feel emotionally is a fact for you. You don't question the validity of your emotions. You don't tell yourself not to feel what you feel.

To respect and validate one's own emotions, a person needs to know what emotions actually are. As a therapist, I ask my patients what they feel emotionally all the time, but for many of them, it's hard to identify what they actually feel. We live in a culture that encourages emotional repression; as a result, people find it difficult to know what they feel emotionally. When I ask my patients what they feel, they usually respond with what they *think,* not what they *feel.* I might ask a patient, "So when your wife talks to you that way when you forget what she told you, how does that affect you emotionally?" Usually the patient will respond with some type of statement about what he thinks, such as, "I feel that she shouldn't talk to me that way. I feel like she is talking to me like a child." In both of these responses, the patient believes he is communicating his emotions, but there is no mention of any emotion. He uses the phrase "I feel," but no emotional words follow. What he is really expressing is his thoughts or judgments, but not emotion.

When trying to identify your emotions, it's best to try to use only one-word descriptions, such as angry, hurt, sad, pleased, happy, or scared. These are a few words that can describe a person's emotional experience. As a therapist, I am looking for these words when I ask the question, "How does that make you feel?" Learning to identify these emotional words is a process of awareness that anyone can follow if they so desire, regardless of gender or age. I have had experience with people who had only about a three-word emotional vocabulary, but who developed a more extensive list of words to describe their emotions over time.

I often ask clients how they feel emotionally, and they will answer that they feel bad or good. It is so common for people to view the terms *bad* or *good* as if they are human emotions. The truth is that these words are value judgments, not human emotions. For example, when someone says they feel bad, I will ask them again if they feel "bad," what do they really feel? This may irritate them a little bit, but then they will usually express a real emotion like sadness or guilt. The goal is to be as accurate as you can about what you truly feel emotionally.

Once individuals identify what they feel emotionally, then the next step is to give that emotion validity. What this means is that individuals believe that how they feel emotionally is a fact, that is, that there is no question or debate as to the validity of what they feel. They don't believe that they need to defend or justify why they feel the way they do, it's just how they feel emotionally. When individuals are able to validate their own emotional truth, they won't tolerate being intimately involved with someone who doesn't share their same belief or respect of emotions.

When I hear the saying, "You have to love yourself before you can love someone else," it sounds great. But what does it mean? In practical terms, when a person respects and validates their own emotions, they will be involved only with someone who thinks the same way. However, if someone doesn't respect their own emotions, then most likely they will allow themselves to be treated with emotional disrespect by another person, which I don't consider a very loving relationship. It is critical that a person respects their own emotions if they want to have a healthy, successful, loving relationship.

PSYCHOLOGICAL BOUNDARIES: ONE KEY TO ALL THREE INTIMACIES

The use of the term boundaries is a relatively new concept. It's one of those psychological buzzwords that are used in popular culture. For the layperson, it's a rather vague concept. Having boundaries in the physical world is not new: neighbors have fences separating their property; countries have borders separating their land. When these boundaries are respected, people usually live in peace; but when these boundaries aren't respected, people and countries go to war. In the same way, people have boundaries separating their psychological space. These boundaries are invisible, but they exist nonetheless. When these boundaries are respected, people get along a lot better in relationships.

The issue for individuals is their ability to establish these boundaries in their daily interactions with others. This becomes especially important in the context of an intimate relationship. Having the confidence that you can establish boundaries in your personal life is the key to falling in love. This confidence allows a person to have that sense of abandon and vulnerability that is so essential to experiencing both emotional and sexual intimacy to the fullest.

In explaining the concept of establishing psychological boundaries in relationships, I like to use the metaphor of what it's like to ski. One of the most crucial abilities in skiing is having the confidence that you know how to stop, preferably on a dime. When skiers point their skis down the mountain and gravity starts to pull them down faster and faster, they are experiencing the rush of skiing. They are "letting go to the mountain" as opposed to resisting and fighting the pull of gravity. Resistance is stressful, exhausting, and not a lot fun. What allows skiers to let go is the confidence that when they become uncomfortable with their experience, they can put the edges of their skis into the hill to slow down or stop if that's what they choose. They are in control the whole time. They choose to let go to the thrill of abandon or to stop to feel comfortable if they are starting to get out of control.

In a relationship, the equivalent of letting go to the hill when skiing is that sense of falling in love. Letting go emotionally in a relationship is very scary if a person doesn't have that sense of having control over what happens to them; that is, they don't have the sense they can set a boundary when they are feeling uncomfortable, or if they do set a boundary that it will be respected. This inability to set boundaries becomes a major block to forming an intimate relationship.

Some people create physical boundaries because they can't establish psychological ones. An example of this is a couple who have a long distant relationship. They put a lot of mileage between themselves, and when they get together, it's incredibly passionate and intimate. They can only tolerate this high level of togetherness for a short time. Boundaries that chronically fail to keep people separated enough are typically described as enmeshed, which means they begin to lose their sense of self in the relationship. This occurs because they are unable to set psychological boundaries and generally are afraid of creating conflicts in the relationship. The way they reestablish their sense of self is to return to their respective homes many miles away from each other. On the surface, this type of relationship might seem difficult and painful, but it keeps the people involved psychologically safe.

Many times this same thing is going on with a single person who has a long-term affair with someone who is married. They complain about how painful it is to be alone so much of the time, and that the person they're involved with says they are going to get a divorce, but doesn't seem to be in a big hurry to do so. On the surface, why would this single person stay in this type of relationship given that they experience so much frustration and loneliness at not being able to spend more time with their lover? The answer lies in understanding the concept of boundaries. The fact that their lover is married and not available provides a certain boundary that keeps them apart, which in turn provides a certain protection against losing their true sense of self. Usually the individual isn't conscious of this safety reason, but it is the only psychological reward I can see for paying such a high price for remaining in this type of relationship.

This pattern can sometimes be seen with the kind of relationships women form with gay men. Gay men represent no threat to the women's sexual boundary so they can relax around them and open up and have greater emotional intimacy because there is no chance that this intimacy will develop into anything sexual, which they might find threatening or conflicting.

The daughter or son who hasn't psychologically cut the cord with their parents also has boundary problems. If the parents believe that they have unhampered access to their adult child's life, the married child's relationship with their spouse will be affected. The spouse will feel as if they are married to two people: one is the adult spouse, and the other is a child who still hasn't psychologically broken away from their parents' control and influence. This isn't a true commitment to the marriage. A choice has to be made in setting boundaries with your parents. They may become upset with any boundaries to their relationship with their adult child; but they have to respect that their child is now an adult and they no longer have any control over how their child leads their life.

SETTING PSYCHOLOGICAL BOUNDARIES

Now that you understand the importance of setting psychological boundaries the question remains, how do you set boundaries in the reality of daily life? I teach this skill every day to my clients and students; but our culture doesn't really teach how to set boundaries except when it comes to our sexual lives. We are encouraged to set all the boundaries we want when it comes to sexual activity, but outside our sex lives, little is said or encouraged. In fact, I think setting boundaries is discouraged in our society.

I try to make psychological concepts such as setting boundaries simple, so people will have an easier time implementing the new skill or behavior into their everyday lives. Simplifying the application of psychological concepts doesn't mean that they will be easy to apply. Some emotional issues may still inhibit their application, but simplifying the process definitely helps.

The basic boundary application process deals with the emotions of comfortable versus uncomfortable. These two emotions can be the basis of how to set a psychological boundary. Just ask yourself the question, "Are you comfortable or not with whatever is being proposed?" These two emotions are your guides in life. They will tell you what is true and right for you. This may not be the same for someone else; but that's okay, because you are learning to love yourself and take care of yourself in a world where others may not care about how you feel emotionally. But you do—at least I hope so.

People are always asking me what I want. Do I want Chinese food or Mexican food for dinner? Do I want to go camping or to stay in a hotel? Which table do I want in a restaurant? On and on it goes. When I hear these questions, the first thing I ask myself is how I feel. If I am not comfortable, I don't move forward. That's how I set a boundary. Listening to and accepting my emotion of comfort gives me the power to set the boundary between others and myself. My emotions are a fact; I don't have to debate their validity, and I don't even have to know why I feel the way I do to give them validity.

If you love another adult, would you want them to do something that they are not comfortable doing? I wouldn't. The price tag for deciding to move forward and not listening to their own emotions is too high. The usual price is resentment, which will later manifest itself in the relationship in some unhealthy way. This also doesn't take into account the unhealthy effect repressed resentment has on the individual, both physically and psychologically.

How many women have sex with a partner when they aren't comfortable participating? Way too many, unfortunately. They participate for all kinds of reasons: "It's just not worth the hassle if I say no and stick to my boundary;" "If I don't participate, he will get upset and pout for days"; "If I say no, he might find someone else and leave me." For these kinds of reasons, the woman does something that she doesn't really want to do, but she sets it up as if she doesn't have a choice. The consequence is that she ends up with a lot of resentment, which is directed at the sexual experience. Eventually, she will lose her sexual desire and most likely, her partner will judge her negatively for her lack of interest—all because she didn't set a sexual boundary within her relationship in the beginning.

Chapter Three

The Two Requirements for a Successful Long-Term Relationship

**"I don't like you, but I love you
seems I'm always, thinking of you
oh, oh, oh, you treat me badly
I love you madly
you really got a hold on me"   —Smokey Robinson**

Interviewers often ask me what makes for success in a long-term rela-
tionship like marriage. In the past, my answers were good communication, shared values, mutual respect, or the ability to resolve conflicts.
These are important ingredients for creating a successful relationship.
However, after years of practicing relationship therapy and counseling,
I now believe that there are two basic personal requirements that both
partners need to fulfill to have a long-lasting intimate relationship.
Once these requirements are met, the basic psychological foundation is
established. Although this is by no means a guarantee, it sure increases
the odds of having a successful relationship. Both of these conditions
also allow an adult to fully love himself or herself and to establish better
self-esteem.

It is easier to fulfill these requirements early in adult life,
especially before someone gets married. This is not to say that these
requirements can't be accomplished later in life or after marriage; it's
just a lot harder.

The first requirement is that individuals have the confidence
that they can take care of themselves **economically** in the world: as
adults, they can financially support themselves by doing some type of

work so they can pay all their basic bills for rent, food, clothing, and utilities. They don't need another adult for money. This confidence isn't about living a fancy lifestyle, but more about their ability to survive on their own.

The second requirement is that individuals have the confidence that they can take care of themselves **emotionally**. They are not afraid to live alone. They don't have to like living alone or want that lifestyle, but they know that they can be alone without being in a significant relationship. They know how to take care of their basic needs, such as cooking, cleaning, and shopping— the basic domestic needs that may have been provided by their mother when they were kids. Taking care of yourself emotionally also means that you have created an emotional support system. This usually involves a network of friends who can meet some of their basic emotional needs, such as support or companionship.

When one or both of these basic requirements are not fulfilled, and an individual becomes involved in a committed intimate relationship, problems occur as a result, and a **dependent** relationship is created.

DEPENDENCY: ITS IMPACT ON SELF-LOVE AND INTIMACY

'Cause that's not love
Love don't feel that bad
That's not love
It don't feel that sad
No that's not love
'Cause you don't feel good inside
I don't know what it is
But that's not love —Keb' Mo'

In the first part of the twentieth century, it was more common for a wife to be dependent on her husband financially, and for her to take care of him emotionally, like his mother may have done when he was a child. This mutuality of dependency was the traditional marital arrangement up until about the late sixties or early 1970s, when some women started to question this arrangement. When social and economic changes occurred and the divorce rates skyrocketed, this type of arrangement started to fall apart and seemed antiquated.

Within the traditional marriage arrangement, there was a blending of two basic psychological concepts: love and dependency. When you loved someone, being dependent on that person was part of the arrangement. This worked because few people got divorced, and being on your own as an adult generally occurred only as a result of the death of a spouse, usually later in life. As a widow, others would come to support you, but if you got divorced, you were stigmatized.

With today's high divorce rate, married people are well aware that they could be single at anytime. At some level, they know that they are at risk of being on their own in the adult world, no matter how much they would like to repress this possible reality. For an individual who is dependent either economically or emotionally, the idea of being on his or her own is especially frightening. It is this fear of being alone that causes psychological havoc in the relationship.

The basic question is how can an adult truly love himself or herself if they are dependent on another adult either economically or emotionally? It's normal for a child to be dependent on their parents for both of these needs. If an adult finds himself or herself in a dependent relationship, their self-worth will be compromised. At either a conscious or an unconscious level, the individual will resent himself or herself for being in a dependent situation. This self-judgment makes self-love impossible.

It's true that when a person is in a marital relationship, they are dependent on another person for their basic emotional needs or perhaps financial support, but this dependency is temporary. If their spouse leaves the relationship for whatever reason, they will be able to take care of themselves. An example of this would be a woman who has a successful dental practice, but has to stop working because she just had a baby and is going on maternity leave. During this period, she is dependent on her husband's income for her financial security. If during this time he decides to leave her for another woman, she is not dysfunctionally dependent, because she can always go back to her dental practice for financial support.

Dependency becomes a problem when there is no fallback position, no "Plan B" if a person is suddenly on their own in the adult world. Many of the clients I work with who are married don't even want to acknowledge the idea of being on their own. It's too scary to go there. Again, this fear of abandonment also plays a major role in creating havoc in the development of intimacy in a long-term relationship.

THE FEAR OF ABANDONMENT: ITS IMPACT ON INTIMACY FORMATION

Dependency in all its forms has as a by-product the fear of abandonment: the dependent's fear of being alone in the adult world. A self-loving, healthy adult has the confidence that if abandonment occurs, they will survive and thrive again. They can withstand the emotional hit of loss. They may not like it or want it to happen, but if the loss occurs, they know deep down they will be okay.

However, someone who is emotionally or economically dependent doesn't have this basic adult confidence. Their security is at risk. It's as if their survival is at stake. They react like a child rather than as an adult. On an emotional level, their development may have been blocked during their childhood because of some type of psychological experience related to their parents or their use of drugs or alcohol. Chronological age and emotional development don't usually align with adults who have dependency issues. You may have a husband who is 35 years old chronologically, but emotionally he may still be a teenager.

Because of this lack of development, the adult who is dependent has two basic problems that affect their ability to form an intimate relationship. The first is that they are not willing to interact in ways that put them at any psychological **risk** within the relationship. Without taking any risk, it's impossible to form a loving, intimate relationship. Taking a psychological risk or making oneself vulnerable emotionally is the essential cornerstone to creating an intimate relationship. Without risk, there can be no in love, just coexistence, roommates. It's as simple as that.

A relationship where no risk is taken may look stable or even ideal from the outside looking in, but when viewed from behind closed doors there exists little emotional or sexual intimacy. Sexual frequency is usually infrequent. There is little conflict between the couple because one or both of the partners can't risk rocking the boat because conflict could lead to divorce and the dreaded fear of abandonment.

One or both of the partners represses their true desires, so there is no conflict. The dependent individual chooses to have harmony over the truth of what they want or feel emotionally. There is no real intimate communication. They just say things that will avoid a negative outcome. Whatever communication they express is internally examined to evaluate the risk level of sharing the information. In the corporate world, this strategic approach to communication is important, but to live this way in your personal life is extremely stressful, to say the least. Without truth, how can any real intimacy exist? What exists is a false reality, which kills the passion within the relationship. This false sense of reality also has a major negative psychological impact on the individual, whose personal life is defined by this need for a fake harmony. I will discuss this impact in detail later in the book.

RESENTMENT POISONS THEIR LOVE

The second problem that exists for adults who are dependent is the development of a great deal of resentment. This resentment develops because at some level of consciousness, they hate being in a dependent relationship as an adult. They resent the fact that their partner has some type of control over their security, either financially or emotionally, and that their partner can make or break their world in this way.

This resentment poisons the love between the couple. It may not be a problem when the relationship is just beginning. In fact, the dependency could feel very loving and warm. It feels like you are being taken care of by your partner, but in a parental way, as opposed to a relationship as equal adults who can take care of themselves. Over time, both individuals begin to resent this dependent care giving—both the giver and the receiver.

How can you love someone that you have so much unresolved resentment toward? The answer is you can't. Resentment gets in the way. It may be expressed in different ways, but resentment blocks intimacy, passion, and love. Many times, for example, unexpressed resentment manifests itself in the form of indifference, complacency, or boredom. The atmosphere between such a couple is emotionally cold. There may be little sexual frequency between the couple. They become roommates who share a common space.

The resentment can also be manifested in constant arguing and power struggles over control of the relationship. These power struggles can become very destructive to the relationship and for the individuals involved. Dependency can become very ugly; the worst example of this is domestic violence.

The irony of a dependent relationship is that those involved will tell you that they love each other, even though their interaction is so hurtful. How can they use the word love in this context? How can they love someone who treats them in such an unloving way? They might say that they have a love/hate relationship. I don't understand how you can hate a person and love them at the same time. You can't love only a part of someone. You have to love the whole person, not just a part of them if you live with them 24/7. When you love someone, you need to be able to accept both their assets and their liabilities.

What people call a love/hate relationship is what I call a need/hate relationship. They are not in this type of relationship out of love, but more because of their dependency on the other person, either emotionally or financially. Dependents/addicts will put up with all kinds of self-degradation and self-abuse to take care of their dependency. Hence, there exists no self-love.

In a therapy session, a client may tell me that their lover treats them in a verbally abusive manner, and that they don't trust them to tell the truth. They feel awful, and their self-esteem is trashed by being in the relationship. The obvious question is why do they stay in this type of relationship? Their answer to the question is usually that they "love" their partner even though they feel the way they do and are not treated with respect. Earlier in my career, I was generally dumbfounded with this type of response, but now I understand. I always wondered how a person could love someone like this and stay in this type of relationship. Usually this type of individual doesn't love himself or herself, and they don't have any real sense of what love actually entails. The idea of leaving the relationship is so threatening that they will allow this type of treatment. They use the word love, but the truth is it's all about dependency of some kind. They stay in the relationship out of fear of being on their own as an adult. Their fear overrides whatever anger or hurt they might experience. They might complain to everyone who will listen about their situation; but when confronted about making some kind of change, they usually find all kinds of reasons to stay the course.

This resistance to change can be very frustrating for anyone who cares about someone who is in this type of addictive relationship. All you can do is watch and listen, or play hardball and give the consequence that if they don't leave the unhealthy situation, you will stop interacting with them. Otherwise, in a way you are enabling them to continue what they are doing by not giving them the consequence of their continued interaction. It is especially difficult give consequences when you care about the person involved.

CIRCLE OF VIOLENCE

Another factor that plays a role in the inability for a dependent person to break out of an addictive relationship is something called the "circle of violence." This is a pattern in relationships where domestic violence is occurring. It's made up of four periods that follow each other in a circle. The first is called the tension-building period where the couple has small resentments that develop from their day-to-day interactions, which they repress and don't really deal with in any constructive manner. These resentments just build and collect over time. This build-up of resentments creates a tension in the atmosphere of the relationship, just like a pressure build-up on a fault line before an earthquake.

After enough tension has built up, the explosion occurs, which is called the acute battering incident. This could be some type of verbally abusive exchange; maybe something thrown against a wall or one of the parties is physically hurt. Something happens that is just over the top for the couple, and in the earlier phases of the cycle it scares the couple in such a way that they never want to go through that type of experience again. Most often, they make their amends with each other.

At this point, the next period comes into play, called the "honeymoon stage." The couple feels close and they want to forget about the incident. They have more sex at this time as a way to put distance between them and the negative experience they just went through. This type of make-up sex is good, but it isn't really making love on an intimate level. It's more about escaping the trauma that just occurred. The couple doesn't take a look at what happened to them and how they got there. They just want to forget the incident. They don't seek professional help, and just sweep the whole thing under the rug and move on with their lives. Whatever caused the problem in the first place is never fully addressed. Because of this avoidance, the cycle is repeated. How long it takes to go through this process varies from couple to couple. Some say they have to go through the cycle seven times before they are able to break free, get out of the situation, and have some type of intervention to break the cycle.

This same cyclic process occurs in an addictive relationship. Generally, the acute battering incident is not some type of physical abuse situation, although it can happen. Most of the time it involves verbal abuse between the couple. They get into a verbal fight, calling each other names with the intention of hurting each other emotionally. This creates a distance between them where they may not speak to each other for days. When their abandonment fear gets so great that they then want to make up, the honeymoon period kicks in, and it's as if everything is all right again. Once their sense of security is back in place, the resentments start to build again and the cycle is repeated. Even when the couple is confronted with this pattern, they may still claim that they love each other. This type of relationship may be what they think love is all about. It just goes with the territory. It isn't until one of them is able to break free because the consequence becomes so severe, such as a situation where the police might be called because the fight got out of hand and someone spends the night in jail. Once the cycle is broken, one of the partners might feel what it's like to be out of this type of dysfunctional dependent relationship. Welcome to the world of emotional sobriety, when the clarity begins, but before it was all a fog.

Understanding the reasons why someone has a dependency problem is not critical in helping them become a functional adult. In the past, therapists spent a lot time in the therapy process rehashing and analyzing what happened in an individual's past to make him or her dependent. This type of insight therapy is interesting, but on its own, it's not going to lead to the solution of the problem. There is a tendency to blame the people in the past and feel like you're a victim, powerless over changing the situation. My therapeutic focus would be on empowerment and the development of confidence over the fear of abandonment.

The degree of dependency that someone might have is not a black and white condition. It's more of a continuum, with someone who is very dependent on one end of the scale to someone who is barely dependent on the other end. Where a person places themselves on this scale relates to their degree of self-love, how they behave in an intimate relationship, and how they react when they find themselves alone. The degree of dependency will have an effect on how they react on the circle of violence referred to earlier.

Chapter Four

Characteristics of a Dependent Personality Type

O ver the years I have noticed that certain common behavioral characteristics are associated with a dependent individual. I used to think that only individuals suffering from alcoholism or drug addictions had these types of characteristics. Now, I see that there is a general addictive personality type, regardless of the addiction or dependency.

The first major characteristic is an individual's inability to take responsibility for their behavior. They find it impossible to take ownership of their actions. They blame others for their behavior. It's not their fault. Someone else made them do it. They drink too much because of the way their wife treats them—not because they might have an alcohol problem. Another example might sound like this: "I wouldn't have hit my wife in the face if she didn't talk to me the way she did." It's always the other person's fault that they act the way they do.

This inability to take personal responsibility makes it difficult, if not impossible, to work with a client like this in a therapeutic context. The client doesn't want to look at their own behavior and try to understand the reasons and motivations for their actions. They just want to talk about the individual that made them act in an inappropriate manner.

This kind of client is in complete denial of how they contribute to any problem. In fact, in their mind, they don't have a problem, so why are they even talking about the issue? Alcoholism is the classic situation, where a person might have two arrests for driving under the influence, but still doesn't believe he has an alcohol problem. Dependents will deny whatever problem they might have that they find threatening to their security. If they are involved in addictive behaviors, their main goal is not to experience their emotions, because it might be too painful and threatening to their lifestyle.

I have had couples come into therapy where the wife tells me how unhappy she in their marriage, and may even be crying. But her husband doesn't understand why they are even seeing a marriage therapist, because he thinks that they have a wonderful marriage and doesn't understand why his wife is so unhappy.

Another common characteristic of dependent personality types is that it's always someone else's fault for whatever problems they might be experiencing. It never has anything to do with them. This is one reason why it's difficult to work with this type of individual in therapy. They are unable to look inward at their own behavior and how it might relate to their difficulties. They tend to play the victim in any situation. Trying to point out what they might be doing to cause their own problems is met with nothing but resistance. They will become defensive and say "yes, but" to whatever you confront them with or whatever you are trying to point out to them. They have an inability to listen to anything they find threatening to their dependency. It's a matter of survival to them and they will defend their position even if it doesn't make any logical sense to anyone else. One way to look at this situation is that you are talking to an adult body, but with a child's mindset. Trying to communicate with this individual can be a very frustrating experience. Don't waste your time or energy tying to get them to see the light, because they are blinded by their dependency. Remember, you can't get someone to change their behavior. Only they can do that. You can only provide consequences to their behavior.

The last classic behavioral trait of dependent personality types is the tendency to be a "Dr. Jekyll and Mr. Hyde." On the one hand, they can start out by being incredibly loving, attentive, and affectionate. They seem to know everything you have ever wanted in a lover, to know what you want and deliver the goods. You feel very intimate with them at first. They are very attentive and interested in the daily occurrences of your life. The relationship seems to be going along very well with few conflicts. Then, seemingly out of nowhere, their behavior changes and they become cold, aloof, and angry. Often, the change occurs over something that they don't like, and then becomes a major issue. All intimacy is lost and they become distant and indifferent toward you and the relationship. This change comes as such a shock and surprise because it is in such contrast to the way the relationship was going before the change took place. Just as quickly as they change from being cold and distant, they can change back to wanting to make up and be close again. The dependent may be apologetic and remorseful and even make promises that they won't act that way again. This cycling back and forth between intimacy and distance can occur over months, or it can change every other weekend.

This is what I call the "flip-flop" of being involved in a dependent relationship, and can be confusing for the person involved with this type of individual. They feel that they are on an emotional rollercoaster. They keep trying to connect with the person they fell in love with, the person who was so loving and caring at first. They tell me that they love their boyfriend or husband, even though they tell me how badly they get treated when their partner flips to the negative side. I ask them: "You love a person like this?" And they answer with an empathic "Yes." "How can you love him?" "He is so disrespectful, but I do. I love him when he is nice to me." It's as if they block out the cold, angry side of their partner; they compartmentalize who their partner really is to somehow justify why they stay involved in the relationship. I don't think you can love only parts of a person to truly love them. You have to accept the whole person's personality and behavior. Usually a dependent individual has a large part of them that's not acceptable.

The degree of animosity that a dependent can show to their lover can also vary. On the mild end of the continuum, his anger and resentment at being a dependent are expressed in the form of complacency, apathy, or indifference. Publicly, he may seem like the proverbial nice guy. He may be very involved with the children and the community. He may go to all of the kids' activities: soccer, baseball, swim meets, and so on. The women in the neighborhood might use him as a base of comparison for their own husbands. So he has great curb appeal, but behind closed doors, it is a whole different story. The operative word is boring. He brings little or no emotional life to the relationship. It's all hidden and shut down. His whole goal is harmony and peace in his family life. No conflict. So there is no realism, no truth of emotion or passion. His wife is not his lover, but more like a roommate who shares common space, and together they try to fulfill their children's needs. They may be good parents together, but that's about all.

His wife doesn't understand what's the matter. She is incredibly frustrated by the situation. She wants her husband to be her lover in all aspects of that role. The couple's sex life is barely occurring—once a month if that. The wife is always the one to initiate sex. Sexual frequency is a real conflict between them, and when they have confronted the issue, they always end up in the same place. Promises are made to try harder, to make changes that will bring about greater intimacy. After a while, though, the "talk and the walk" don't come together, and the dependent's credibility is lost; his promises have no meaning.

Not only does this couple have little sexual intimacy, they rarely go out on a date alone without other people being around. Outside of work life, they do everything with their children. It's all about the family—as if there is no marriage in the family. The marriage relationship has lost its identity. It has become enmeshed with the family. Unfortunately for this couple, the marriage is the foundation of the family, and when the marriage dies and falls apart, so does the family.

The couple may say defensively that they don't know anyone they could trust or feel comfortable to leave their children with. Or they respond by saying that they can't afford to pay a babysitter. When they tell me that they can't afford a babysitter, I always think of the hourly rate of a divorce lawyer. There is no comparison on the investment return ratio. By not investing the time and money into their marriage relationship, they are being negligent and allowing their relationship to die out on the vine. They may not do this consciously or intend to treat their marriage in this manner, but from the outside that is what is happening.

The dependent lives in a state of denial, not realizing that if they don't take care of their marriage, it will fall apart and they will end up in the "singles' market." Both partners may believe on a conscious or unconscious level that marriage is "till death do us part, so don't worry, we will always be together." What a nice fantasy in today's world of divorce. It isn't a pretty picture when their denial is broken and reality sets in, changing their lives. It can be pretty devastating, but that's what is sometimes required to make these personal changes.

The dependent may tell their partner that they love them very much, but somehow their behavior doesn't speak to this fact. They will be emphatic when their partner threatens them in some way about the future of their relationship. Once the threat is removed from the atmosphere, the dependent reverts back to their usual indifferent behavior. For the dependent, what's important is not how emotionally intimate they are with their partner, but how secure they feel about the stability of their relationship. As long as their partner is accessible to them, they can rest easy.

So far, I have discussed the dependent whose style is to repress his or her anger at being dependent, but on the other end of the spectrum is the dependent who acts out their anger in a more dramatic fashion. The relationship can be going along fairly well when suddenly and unexpectedly the dependent reacts in an outburst of anger. Usually they get very loud in their speech and become quite agitated in their behavior. Someone else is always to blame for their behavior. On the surface, their anger is usually related to the perception that the security in their relationship is being threatened.

When their fear of abandonment emerges, this type of dependent reacts aggressively by trying to control their partner in some way. They attack their partner's actions, assuming that their partner intends to hurt them. They become very jealous of the opposite sex and try to cut off their partner from having contact with whoever they perceive as a threat to their sense of security. Do not mistakenly view this reaction of jealousy as an act of romantic love. It has nothing to do with love; it's all about power and control. They want to control their partner's actions that they see as threatening.

They use all types of control methods to keep their partner from leaving them. Dependents are generally very toxic to their partners' self-esteem. At first they may tell you how wonderful you are to seduce you into having an intimate relationship with them; but once they believe they have you hooked, they start to change their tune. They start to be critical of whatever part of their partner they perceive as a vulnerability or insecurity. If it's a husband, he may make comments about his wife's appearance, usually about her weight. The wife wants to please her husband, but after a while she begins to feel frustrated or hopeless. She is never good enough for him. The bar of expectation keeps moving. After a period of time, she may just give up trying to meet his expectations and then start to believe that there is something wrong with her. Her self-esteem starts to plummet. He may be critical of the way she dresses in public or how much makeup she wears. He is fearful of her being attractive to other men, so he wants to shut down her sexuality. But at the same time, he may criticize her for not being sexy for him. This is crazy-making behavior, a total double bind for his wife.

A wife who is dependent may also do the same thing to her husband—she may find his vulnerabilities and judge him as well. She may be critical of how much money he makes or the type of work he does for a living. Her husband may feel that he can never make enough to satisfy his wife's needs. She may also be critical of his male friends, because they represent a threat to her need to control him. They might make him feel good about himself through their support and undermine her efforts to cripple him psychologically.

You might ask why someone would want to destroy their lover's self-esteem. You would think that they would want to support and bolster their partner's self-esteem because they say they love their partner. The question is, do they really love their partner or do they need them? The dependent's basic fear of abandonment is at the root of the problem. Their fear is that if their partner starts to develop high self-esteem and confidence that they won't want to be involved with them anymore and will leave. As a result, dependents are on a mission—either on an unconscious or eventually on a conscious level—to destroy their partners' self-esteem. They don't admit to this mission, but if you look at a lot of their communication, it is very judgmental. They may offer a compliment so they can defend themselves that they support their partner, but they will take the compliment away on the backside with some type of criticism.

Male dependents tend to attack their girlfriend's or wife's sexuality, and often feel threatened if their partner feels good about herself sexually. Their lover's sexuality may have been what they found most attractive and positive about her in the beginning; but after they have some type of commitment within the relationship, the criticism begins. Little negative comments, well positioned for maximum impact, start to be communicated about how their partner dresses or how she might have some imperfection physically, like carrying too much weight in certain areas of her body. The qualities that male dependents desired in the beginning of the relationship are the ones they start to tear down and destroy after a period of time.

This shift in attention is very confusing to the woman. The female partner is often blindsided by this change in their partner's behavior, and may react to this criticism by trying to please their partner by striving even harder to meet his ever-rising expectations. But she continually fails at trying to meet his expectations because they are generally unrealistic. As she begins to fail in meeting her husband's expectations, her self-esteem starts to plummet.

She gives him all the power to decide her worth, because without his approval she believes that she will lose his love and eventually he will leave her for someone better. This belief is exactly what her dependent partner wants her to think. The reality is that he won't leave her—he's too dependent—but he doesn't want her to know that fact. The bottom line is that being involved with a dependent individual over time will destroy an individual's self-esteem as a being a lover, spouse, or even a parent.

DEPENDENCY AND GENDER

When it comes to dependency issues there are gender differences. But neither sex has a monopoly on the dependent personality. Where the dependency differences exist between the sexes, it is more a function of cultural conditioning. There are many women and men who get involved with addictive substances and behaviors. Where it becomes a gender issue is when we are looking at two particular dependencies: economic and emotional. These two dependencies were discussed at the beginning of chapter three in relation to self-love and intimacy.

Who is more likely to be economically dependent in our society? Typically, women seem to fit this role. Traditionally, our culture conditioned them to stay home and raise the children. They weren't encouraged to become professionals or develop skills that would put them in the work force. This was the old message, but today this has all changed. We still don't have equal pay for equal work between men and women, but the number of economically dependent women has radically shifted. Men are taught from a very early age that they must work and get a job—that's what being a male is all about in our culture. Men have usually developed a skill set that enables them to make money and take care of themselves by the time they reach adulthood. If they haven't, they are judged as inadequate and not real men.

And when I ask who is more inclined to be emotionally dependent between men and women, usually the answer I get is also women. The popular perception is that women are generally more dependent, both economically and emotionally. Women are perceived as being emotionally dependent because they are more emotionally expressive. Women tend to be more communicative about their emotions than men are, but does this actually make them dependent? The answer is no. Just because they express their emotions doesn't make them dependent. Another reason that women are seen as emotionally dependent is that they seem to need more emotional intimacy in their relationships than men do. Does this need for intimacy make them dependent? Not really—it just underlines the fact that they are generally much more comfortable with intimacy than men.

From all of my professional experience, though, I don't view women in general as being emotionally dependent when compared to men. Women are taught how to take care of themselves and others on an emotional level. Women create emotional support through all their networks of interacting with other women. Women talk to other women about their emotions and personal problems and feel supported by this process. If a woman is single, she is in a better position to take care of herself emotionally. Her struggle—if she has one—is economic survival. "For better or worse, women are less dependent on men or the institution of marriage....Younger women understand this better, and are preparing to live larger parts of their lives alone or with non-married partners. For many older boomer and senior women, the institution of marriage did not hold the promise they might have hoped for, growing up in an 'Ozzie and Harriet' era," according to William H. Frey, a demographer with the Brookings Institution, a research group in Washington.

The individual who is generally emotional dependent in a relationship is often the male. Men in this culture are not taught or prepared to be on their own emotionally. The concept of taking care of themselves emotionally seems foreign to them. I have asked hundreds of men after their wives have left them, "How are you going to take care of yourself on an emotional level now that she is gone?" They look at me with an expression of disbelief, like "What are you talking about?" They don't have a clue. The way they take care of themselves emotionally is to find a woman. It can be their mother if she is alive, a girlfriend, or another wife. If they can't find a woman, then they take care of their emotions with alcohol, marijuana, prescription drugs, or any substance that takes away their emotional pain. If they don't use these substances then they stay busy with lots of work or they go to the gym and work out a lot, thinking that physical exercise will fulfill them emotionally.

A male will not generally develop an emotional support system of friends, male and female, who he can turn to and share his personal emotional experience. He keeps his pain and loneliness hidden. He can only share superficially when he is in any social situation where he might be interacting with others. His sense of what it means to be a male in this culture—someone who isn't vulnerable or has no emotional needs—keeps him bottled up and repressed. This inability to share only adds to his sense of loneliness, alienation, and pain.

The idea of a man admitting that he is emotionally dependent on a woman is difficult to imagine, because it goes against his masculine self-image of being independent of others in fulfilling his needs. The theory is that the more a man professes he doesn't need a woman in his life, the more he does. In psychology textbooks, this is called counter dependency. This concept has held true in my work, because the men I see as "acting hard-ass" or "macho" in relation to the women in their life really fall apart emotionally when their partner leaves them. They act in a cocky manner as long as they have a woman standing by them or they feel that they still have control over their partner. Sometimes this situation is characterized by the phrase, "If you're leaving, don't let the door hit you in the ass on the way out." When the man saying this realizes that his wife or girlfriend was serious and isn't coming back, he falls apart and will do anything to get her back again. How quickly his attitude changes when he senses abandonment—potential or actual.

When men find themselves alone emotionally, they have a great opportunity for personal growth. They are at the crossroads of personal development, no matter what their chronological age may be. They can choose the old childlike path of seeking a woman they can be emotionally dependent on again, knowing that it feels familiar and comforting for the moment, but they are repeating a dysfunctional pattern, and a pattern they have probably repeated many times in their life. They know it's a pattern, but they either don't know how to break out of it or don't want to out of fear. Or they can try a new road that is scary but is the direction of growth and real change: the path of learning to live on their own without the assurance or security that they have *one* woman in their life they can count on to be there for them if they are alone.

What this path entails is learning to create their own emotional support system where they have created and invited people into their life, both men and women, who can fulfill their emotional needs at different times and in different ways. This breaks down the need for dependency on one woman to be there for them, and if she is gone, they have a backup system so there is no need to panic. They will survive the loss. A male who has achieved this sense of confidence of being able to be on his own emotionally is truly in a place where he can say that he doesn't *need* one woman, but instead he *wants* to be with a woman. The distinction in this statement is the difference between need and want. Need implies the lack of choice; it's non-negotiable, whereas the use of want in this context implies choice. Without this choice, there exists dependency and ultimately resentment or even hatred—both toward the woman they're dependent on, and toward themselves for being dependent as an adult. This resentment is the basis for so much intimacy dysfunction in many relationships and makes the formation of true love of self or of another impossible.

THE ANTIDOTE TO MEN'S EMOTIONAL DEPENDENCY: MY OWN STORY

Besides developing an emotional support system as an antidote to being emotionally dependent, it's critical that a male develops qualities within himself that he might define as feminine. This was true in my own case, and I have seen the same issue with many men I have worked with in therapy over the years. When I was about twenty-five, I found myself single as an adult for the first time in my life. I lived in my own house without having a steady girlfriend or even a roommate. Alone. I was conscious of what I was trying to do, which was to live alone without a woman in my life other than my mother, who lived four hundred miles away. I lived this way for about six months, but really didn't enjoy this lifestyle, so I decided to get a roommate to share my house. I needed more of a social life and thought that living with someone else would make my life fuller. I thought at the time that I should be able to live alone and not need a roommate, but this wasn't the case. I needed people in my life, which is the kind of personality I have. The trick is not to need just one person.

I found a male roommate, Doug, who had a great stereo system and was a manager of a local restaurant, which I thought would give me great access to lots of women I could date. To my amazement, when he moved in the first thing he did was to change his bedroom into what seemed to me like a living room. He put in a peaceful fish tank; Navajo rugs on the walls, along with hanging ferns and stuffed chairs, which all resulted in a very comfortable environment.

From his room you went next door to my bedroom, which had a bed, dresser, and a poster on the wall. My room was devoid of any femininity. It was cold, sterile, and basically uninviting. I remember at the time that I was waiting to get involved with a woman and then she could move in and live with me. She could then decorate our bedroom and the rest of the house.

In reality, I didn't really like the women who wanted to start helping me decorate telling me what I could do to my house. I felt they were trying to change my environment and me, and it felt like my mother was living with me, which wasn't much of a turn-on. On the other hand, the women that I was attracted to—usually independent women, somewhat emotionally aloof—didn't want any part of taking care of my emotional needs. They didn't want to be like my mother to me, and weren't interested in being involved with me.

The net result was that the women who wanted to be with me I rejected, and the women I was attracted to wanted no part of having a relationship with me. The bottom line was that I ended up being without anyone significant in my life at that time. In the meantime, I got to hear my roommate with all of his girlfriends hanging out in his bedroom down the hall. This experience was very frustrating to say the least. On a conscious level, I was telling all my friends that I wanted to be in a relationship and asking if they knew of anyone that I could date. The truth was that I wasn't ready to be in a committed relationship, and on an unconscious level, I was setting it up so that I ended up being alone until I was ready psychologically. I was still hurting from a past relationship and didn't trust myself with getting seriously involved again, even though I didn't know this fear existed on a conscious level.

With the help of a wonderful therapist, I was able to discover that until I developed the feminine within my own psychological makeup, I wasn't going to be attractive to the type of woman I wanted in my life. I used to tell her that I wanted Karen back in my life, and then I would be happy. She would say, "No you don't, you want the Jane in you." I would say, "What are you talking about? I want to be with Jane again." She would explain, "You don't want to be with Karen; you were unhappy when you lived with her. You want what Karen represented—having a female complete you psychologically. Without her, you are incomplete and off balance."

Well, that was hard to hear at first, but then it started to make sense. If I was complete with both a feminine and masculine balance within my own psychological makeup, then I didn't *need* a woman to complete me. I could say then with confidence that I *want* to be with a woman to share my life's experiences without the dependency and fear of abandonment ruling my decisions and behavior within a relationship. The woman I was with would have no power over my emotional well-being overall.

I developed my feminine side by doing all the things in life that I looked to a woman to do for me—such as cooking, cleaning, laundry, decorating, and learning to dress myself in an appropriate way. If a woman did any of these activities for me it was a gift, something I could appreciate, not something that I was dependent on her doing for me. I learned to nurture myself instead of looking to a woman to do that for me the way my mother did. What this meant was creating activities that gave me pleasure in a healthy way instead of enduring pain and emptiness, which was perceived as the more masculine thing to do within our culture.

I learned to sit on the beach, relax, and recharge my batteries, and not to feel guilty that I was "wasting time" because I wasn't accomplishing anything. It was so hard to give myself pleasure, outside of the sexual area. I could spend money on a woman for entertainment, nice dinners, or expensive trips. To treat myself in the same manner was out of the question. I would spend as little as possible on myself if I were eating out alone. I would buy the least expensive clothes I could get away with and still look presentable. It wasn't a question of having enough money; it was more about whether I deserved the quality. However, my attitude changed as I realized that self-nurturance was a good concept because it made me less dependent on having a woman in my life.

It also showed me and others that I loved myself. Why would I treat a woman I was interested in having a relationship with in a very caring, loving manner, but then treat myself as if I didn't matter? When it came to me, I could make do with less and I could get by with the least expensive item or experience. What kind of message did this type of behavior send to a potential lover? What it told her was that I didn't really love myself. This would tend to make me attractive to co-dependent women, who wanted to take care of me just like my mother. Of course, this would feel good at first because it was what I associated with love and comfort. It was something I was looking for at some level being single and alone out in the adult world. It felt comfortable in the beginning of the relationship, but then I would start to push the woman away, because I would resent the control she applied in her attempt to take care of me. No adult usually responds well to someone trying to control him or her, regardless of the intentions involved. So I would end the relationship, blame the woman for its failure, and go out to try to find another girlfriend that I thought was better than the last one.

This pattern continued for a couple of years until I started to ask myself why these relationships didn't last, and until I stopped blaming the women in the relationship. I then understood that I didn't really want Jane back in my life, just like the therapist was trying to tell me, but that I just wanted a generic woman to take care of me. That's when I developed the confidence to take care of myself. I was then truly free to love a woman for who she was as a person, an individual, and not a service commodity to take care of my emotional needs.

CO-DEPENDENCY AND THE IMPACT ON A RELATIONSHIP

The term co-dependency came into existence sometime in the mid-1990s. Its usage came about because of a popular book titled *Co-dependency No More*, written by Melody Beattie in 1989. Soon the term co-dependency became a part of the popular psychological jargon. When I was in graduate school, we called it "rescuing." The term for someone who was involved with an alcoholic was "co-alcoholic." The term then evolved into co-dependency. Many people use this word, but I am not sure if they know what it really means.

I define co-dependency as a person who takes responsibility for an adult financially, emotionally, sexually, or in any other kind of way. To take responsibility means that they are in charge of what happens, whether good or bad, to another adult. An individual who takes on this sense of responsibility may have good intentions in terms of their behavior, but in reality, this action is dysfunctional.

The reason co-dependency is dysfunctional is because the only people that an adult should be responsible for is a child, because by definition a child is dependent, but an adult is ideally responsible for all aspects of their life. So what develops in a co-dependent/dependent relationship between adults is that they turn their relationship psychologically into a parent/child situation. In the beginning of this type of relationship, things may seem to work, and the couple feels very in love with each other because this sense of being taking care of feels like love and is very familiar given their past experiences, but over time, this relationship will turn into a very unhappy situation.

Why is this? At first, being responsible feels satisfying, but after a while the co-dependent begins to develop a lot of resentment and frustration directed at the dependent individual. The resentment is usually about the fact that their partner is not getting better, which really means that whatever their dependency is regarding, they are not becoming independent or changing. The co-dependent believes at some level that they can change an adult, or that they can "fix" their dependency, whatever that might be. The co-dependent has a false sense of power and control regarding their relationship with others. They become frustrated because their partner isn't changing in the way they think they should. Given that they have the belief they can change the people they are involved with, they try harder to get them to change. They lecture and use logical persuasion to motivate the dependent to change their ways, and in a sense tell them to grow up and be self-reliant. The more they push, the more resistance they get from the person they are trying to change. The co-dependent's efforts, which they believe are made done with good and loving intentions, turn into a major power struggle between the couple. The impact of this power struggle is to shut down any love and intimacy between them. A typical example of this is the fact that you can't get someone sober; only they can clean up their act when they decide to live that way.

I learned firsthand that co-dependency doesn't work in my own life, in my relationship with my father. As a child, I tried to get my father to stop smoking. When I was a child, and then later as an adult, I was fearful that my father was going to die from smoking. He would also cough so violently in public I would be so embarrassed, especially around my friends. So I wanted my father to just stop smoking. I didn't understand addiction at that time, so I thought he could just make that decision and stop. I would steal his cigarettes and throw them out, thinking I could control his smoking. If I saw him smoking I would harass him and confront him and show him very little respect regarding any of his own personal boundaries. I justified these actions by telling myself that I was saving his life, but really, I was selfishly trying to keep him alive so I wouldn't lose him. All these efforts were in vain, because he just kept smoking no matter what I did or said to him. At some point I gave up and said, "If you want to kill yourself smoking there is nothing I can do to stop you." I let go and stopped being co-dependent. Finally, at some point, his doctor was able to tell him that if he didn't stop smoking he was going to die soon and at that point he decided to stop. He died of lung cancer and heart failure about six months later. My fear became a reality, and my father was gone. I am sure that my story is not unique. The pattern is the same, even though the dependency may be different.

So if being co-dependent causes an individual so much resentment and frustration, why would they want to participate in this type of behavior? What is the psychological payoff for the co-dependent? When I confront a co-dependent with this question, they say that there is no payoff, that they don't get anything positive out of being this way in a relationship with a partner. They look at me as if to say, "Are you kidding?" The reality is that there are psychological payoffs to being a co-dependent even if the individual is unaware of them.

The first psychological payoff is a false sense of power and control. If a person believes that they are responsible of another adult, then that puts them in the control position. They believe they have the power to make someone close to them happy or unhappy. They can change them into the person that they think they should be in terms of their behavior or emotional well-being. This false sense of control gives the co-dependent the feeling that they are not vulnerable when they are in a relationship. They think they have the power to change their partner into what works for them.

Another payoff for co-dependent behavior is that it gives the individual a sense of identity and purpose. It gives them a role to play in their life. Their role is being the "caretaker" of others or of one person who generally has some type of dependency problem. The co-dependent in this context believes that they care, and that their effort at taking care of someone else is a positive, loving behavior. They don't see anything wrong with what they are doing; if confronted with their behavior, they will probably become defensive. When the person who is dependent on this co-dependent becomes self-reliant and no longer is living a dependent lifestyle, this shift upsets the co-dependent because they believe they are no longer needed. They have a co-dependent crisis, which involves a loss of identity and purpose to their life. It's not unusual for them to become the dependent, and they can't seem to function in their own life without someone taking care of them.

When I have worked with co-dependent clients and they have learned not to take responsibility for others in a dysfunctional way, they soon realize they started losing most of their friends. It's like when an alcoholic stops drinking and they lose their association with all of their drinking buddies. The foundation of the relationship is taken away and they dissolve. Now the co-dependent is free to enjoy relationships with people who can give back instead of just taking.

One other lesser-known psychological payoff of co-dependency is that it allows the co-dependent to lose themselves in the problems and issues of others or specifically with one dependent individual, like a spouse or friend. The co-dependent in this case is so involved in taking care of the dependent that they don't have time for themselves and their own issues. They don't have time to ask themselves how they feel emotionally about anything; they just get lost in the dependent's constant psychological drama. In a way, it works like a drug, in that it tunes out their own emotional experience and provides an escape from their reality.

As a psychotherapist, I go through a similar experience in dealing with my clients' problems. In listening intently and problem solving their issues, I totally lose track of my own daily problems and feelings. It isn't until I leave the office and start driving home that my own life comes back to my consciousness. The difference is that I am not taking my clients' issues home with me; I set a boundary between the professional and the personal; otherwise, I would be totally burned out in a week. I am not responsible for my clients' lives.

Co-dependency is a way to avoid dealing with something in a person's life that they find threatening. Many times this may be an unhappy marriage that they don't want to confront, or a lack of self-identity. The co-dependent is in denial about this process, and if confronted, they usually become defensive. If the dependent becomes independent and in a sense puts the "co" out of business, then they experience something called a "co-dependent crisis." This is similar to a dependent hitting bottom and having their denial shattered. This crisis can be a positive experience, because it is the best time to help the co-dependent let go of their dysfunctional approach to life, assuming that they are motivated to make a change.

Chapter Five

The Three Selfs: Self-Identity, Self-Esteem, Self-Confidence

There are three terms that start with self that get used a great deal in psychological discussions about learning to love yourself. I think it's important to define what these terms mean, because many times they get confused and misrepresented in common discussions.

SELF-IDENTITY

Often in therapy sessions a client will say, "I have lost my identity; I no longer know who I am; I have lost myself." I could come back and with a flip question and ask, "Where did you leave it?" but that would be inappropriate. The client truly feels that they don't know what they are about any longer; they are unable to define themselves. Usually this occurs when a role they have been playing in their life has come to an end.

When children move out of the house and they begin their own adult lives, the mother may feel that she is no longer needed. Being a mother defined who she was, at least from her perspective. A major void is now created in her daily life, and she feels lost, or has an identity crisis. This situation is often called the "empty nest syndrome."

This same situation can occur for a man who has worked his whole life in a specific career and has defined himself by that career— he sees himself as a lawyer, doctor, or plumber, etc. When he retires from his career, he first has a sense of joy and release, but then the identity crisis starts, and he starts having difficulty with his sense of worth. You can only play so much golf or tennis. There is a phenomenon where an individual works hard at one career and can't wait to retire, but when he finally does, he dies before he is able to enjoy his retirement.

What is self-identity? Is it just being a mother or a carpenter? Not usually. An individual's self-identity is composed of all the roles and interests established at any certain point in their life. At this point in my life, my identity is composed of being a husband, father, friend, teacher, therapist, author, and a tennis player, to name just a few. I will probably develop new roles or interests; therefore, my identity isn't a static position, but is ever changing. The more a person's self-identity is diversified, the more interesting and stable their life will be compared to those who define themselves by only one role or interest.

SELF-ESTEEM

Another term involving self is self-esteem. It is so common for clients to use this term to describe themselves as having high or low self-esteem when I start working with them. When I ask them what they mean by self-esteem, they seem surprised and say, "You know what I mean. The way I feel about myself." What they usually mean is that they have a self-judgment that they are either good or bad overall as an individual. Their belief is usually that they are bad, which translates to low self-esteem. This self-judgment has been a chronic belief over a long period of time, which relates to why they have been depressed, or the self-judgment has developed due to some recent occurrence or event in their life. Clients take these events personally and believe there is something wrong with them. As an outcome of this belief, they develop low self-esteem.

The model for describing self-esteem that works in helping clients build and develop self-esteem is to view it as a set of cognitive beliefs made up of attributes and liabilities relating to one particular part of a person's total identity. One exercise I have a client do is to make a list of the roles and activities that make up their identity, such as being a mother, wife, friend, lover, cook, tennis player, and so forth. After they make the list, I have them take each part of their identity and list the positive attributes that go with that particular role or activity. I ask them to write down the characteristics that make them a good mother or friend, for example. Writing them down on a piece of paper is important, because it makes the belief tangible when you see something in black and white on paper. The belief doesn't just float in and out of an individual's consciousness; it stays right there in their mind in visual terms.

Often someone will say to me that they are depressed and have low self-esteem. I say to them, "Really, why is that?" They respond that they don't know; maybe it's because they don't have a boyfriend and can't seem to meet anyone on the Internet. Then I ask them to pretend that I am interviewing them to work at my company. I want them to tell me why I would want to hire them to be my employee. At that point, they seem to perk up and start telling me their attributes: they get along with other workers, they learn quickly, they are on time to work, and so on. I then ask them to tell me why someone would want to be in a relationship with them, and they seem to go blank or say they don't know. What this illustrates is that they have self-esteem as a worker but are lacking in one particular area of their identity: being a partner in a relationship.

The mistake that so many people make is that they may have poor self-esteem in one area of their identity, but have high self-esteem in many others. Because of this one negative area, they over-generalize their negative belief about their self-esteem and apply it to all areas of their identity, and then lose sight of what's truly occurring. As a psychotherapist, I see many clients who show me real life examples of this cognitive process in action. For instance, the spouse who finds out that their mate is involved in an extramarital affair and believes that they now have no self-esteem left in any aspect of their life. Another common example is when someone loses their job, either by being fired or laid off because of political or economic cutbacks. However this negative event occurs, the individual generally has a lowered self-esteem in all areas that define who they are in this world. When a person has this perception of very low self-esteem, they often have an associated general depression, which is usually the presenting problem when they seek psychological help.

SELF-CONFIDENCE

The last self-term is self-confidence. Many people use this term synonymously with self-esteem, but they are two separate concepts. High self-esteem doesn't necessarily mean that someone will have self-confidence. Self-esteem is a set of beliefs an individual has related to one part of their identity. They don't really know if these beliefs are completely true until they test their beliefs beyond themselves.

Self-confidence means taking one's self-beliefs into the real world to see if they hold true, and if they do, then the self-confidence occurs. Self-confidence is developed through an individual's experience. Usually the experience may occur over repeated occasions. The illustration I like to use for the development of self-confidence is when I learned to ski. I would ski down a difficult ski run and fall down five times. I believed that I was a competent skier. I had good self-esteem in this area, but on this particular run, I didn't have a great deal of self-confidence. So I went back up the ski hill and went down the same run again, but this time I fell down only twice. After repeating this process several more times, I was no longer falling down. I had developed self-confidence on this particular ski run.

In my practice, I see many clients who have been married for many years and now find themselves newly single. They may have self-esteem about being in a new relationship, but they have no confidence in being single. It may have been twenty years since they were in the single world, and things have changed since they were out there dating. They have no confidence and have a great deal of fear of dating again. I usually respond by asking, "How can you have confidence if you are doing something new for the first time?" That's like me thinking I can ski perfectly on the first day out on the slopes. It is normal to be afraid to do something new, but you don't want to let this fear get in the way of developing a new relationship. The key is to allow yourself to make mistakes. After repeated experiences, you will learn the dos and don'ts, and over time you may become self-confident in whatever activity you pursue if you have the appropriate skills and attributes from the outset.

INFLUENCES ON OUR SELF-ESTEEM

When we are born, we essentially have neutral self-esteem. We are born as a blank slate. As we grow up and are socialized within this society, we allow certain powerful forces to influence the formation and development of our self-esteem. To either rebuild and/or change our self-esteem, it's important to understand these influencing forces. Why do we think about ourselves the way we do? How did these beliefs make their way into our psychological makeup?

Parents

When it comes to influencing our sense of self-esteem, our parents or parent figures, such as stepparents or grandparents, have the greatest impact on our self-esteem formation. One reason for this is that they get to us first. A child believes whatever their parents say about them because to a child their parents are the "gods." They know all and are always present in a child's early developing days. A child has no other frame of reference in the world than their parents. They can't check out their parents with others to see if they are right. Therefore, parents hold enormous power in affecting their child's self-esteem.

Another reason parents have so much power in influencing a child's self-esteem is that it's critical to a child to obtain their parents' validation and love. This is because a child needs a sense of security, and with their parents' love and validation, they will feel secure. Children try to get their parents' approval by trying to meet their parents' expectations. Unfortunately, parents who don't have good self-esteem themselves have trouble passing something on to their children what they don't have themselves.

Instead, they use the child's need for validation for their own purposes of power and control over their child. This in turn leaves a very insecure, anxious, and angry child, because the security they seek is never attained. The child doesn't give up seeking the parents' approval. They may take this struggle for validation into their adult life and even all the way to their parents' deathbed: "Please, Dad, tell me I was a success, tell me I was a good son, before you die." It's like a psychological carrot that parents hold out for their child to chase, but never obtain. If parents were to give their child validation, it would put them out of the power and control business. They would have to be on the same level as their grown children: both being equal as adults with neither having any power over the other. In this case, the parents would have to give up their identity as parents interacting with a child, and if they don't have any other real identity in their lives, this loss could be terrifying. If you are an adult and you find yourself still trying to get your parents' validation and approval, it's time to give up the pursuit. It's time to cut the psychological umbilical cord. It's time to get your power back and validate yourself. Just the act of taking your power back and acting like an adult will positively affect your self-esteem.

Another major way that parents validate their children's self-esteem is by evaluating them based on their behavior. Children are judged by their actions, and therefore their actions define their worth. This classic dialogue illustrates the point: "John, you are such a bad boy when you spill milk all over the place."Instead, the parent could use this approach: "You know, John, you are such a wonderful boy, but when you spill milk on the floor it makes such a mess."

So many people experience the first approach. Being loved and validated were connected to how they behaved as children. Not that there is a problem with reinforcing a child's behavior with praise or providing negative consequences for unacceptable behavior; it's just that the validation needs to occur out of a behavioral context. Children need to be loved and validated for the traits they have that are not connected to their actions or the quality of their performance.

A common consequence later in life when a child's self-esteem was connected to how they acted when they were growing up is that they become very defensive verbally when someone close to them has a problem with how they act. They take what that person has to say personally. This usually means that they get emotionally hurt, because to them, their significant other is not just criticizing their behavior; they are attacking them on a personal level. Their behavior and their sense of self are one in the same. When you say something critical or negative about their actions you are saying they as an individual are negative, and they could even take it that you don't love them because of the way they acted.

An example of this pattern might go like this: my wife says that the way I load the dishwasher is totally incorrect, and she gets upset by the way I load the dirty dishes. If I connect my self-esteem to my behavior, most likely I would get upset at her judgment and react by feeling hurt. Then I would likely become verbally defensive, attack back, and defend the way I load the dishwasher, saying that the way she does it is wrong. This is also an example of how small issues get blown into a full-scale personal warfare of attack and defend, and all intimacy is lost over something minor like how to load a dishwasher.

If I don't connect my self-esteem to my behavior, I might take another path. I wouldn't react and become defensive, because I wouldn't take the criticism personally. I would know that the way I load the dishwasher works for me, even though my wife would do it differently. She just has a problem with my behavior and not with me as her husband. She still loves me; she just doesn't like my behavior. An adult who was loved for how they acted when they were a child cannot make this distinction. For them, if you dislike their behavior, you dislike them. I think this is why so many conflicts that couples have over what they call the "small stuff" escalated into major arguments. The conflict switches quickly from something like how to load a dishwasher to questioning the couple's love for each other, which then becomes incredibly emotional.

Many parents validate their child's self-esteem based on what activities they pursue. If a father has a son and dreams of him playing football or some other sport that the father has a passion for, he expects that his son will pursue this passion. If he does, he will get tons of validation for meeting his father's expectations. If he doesn't follow the path his father wants, he is judged in a negative way, and has to struggle to hold on to his dream instead of his father's.

Like many of you, I was always asked that proverbial question when growing up, "So what are you going to be when you grow up, Danny?" If you answered what your parents wanted to hear, then you got all kinds of accolades, but if you said something that they didn't approve of, you were judged and felt awful. I always got the feedback that I was good with my hands because I liked to build models of airplanes and ships. The parent figures in my childhood said that I should become a dentist. So I learned that was the right response to the question about my future. I always got a positive response because I would make a lot of money as a dentist. Making a great deal of money was the important value, not whether or not I would enjoy that kind of work. Gradually, becoming a dentist just became an automatic response, a self-fulfilling prophecy that I didn't question by the time I was in high school and college. I was on the academic track to go to dental school. This career path came to an end after my first quarter as a junior at the University of California. I took a look at my grades and said to myself, "I don't really like the physical sciences classes, and I'm just getting by academically." The class I received an A in was sociology, and I realized that I enjoyed this class. At that moment, I decided to go with how I felt instead of what I should do according to my parents. I will never forget that phone call to mother telling her that I was changing my major from biochemistry to sociology. She was very upset and kept asking, "So what kind of job are you going to get with a sociology degree?" I didn't care about my employment opportunities at that time; I just wanted to start studying something that I had a passion for as opposed to forcing myself academically and not doing well. The rest is history as they say, but making that decision to change directions was one of the great lessons I learned for myself, which was to listen to my own emotional guide instead of the "shoulds" of other people. I see this pattern repeated over and over in the lives of my clients. When an individual starts living for what works for them, as opposed to what their parents want, that individual truly becomes an adult psychologically.

All too often, a child's worth is defined by his or her performance of some type of activity that they pursue in their developing years. It could be how they play a certain sport in high school or being the homecoming queen or being the class president or being the cum laude of their graduating class. You probably remember those individuals when you were in high school. Early in our development, parents defined a child's worth by what we did and not who we were as an individual. What happens when a child is no longer interested or involved in that particular activity their parents want their child to pursue? Will their parents still love and validate them if they don't play football, for example? For a child who is burned out on a particular activity that their parents are still very passionate about, making this change can be very scary.

Growing up in our family of origin, we want our parents approval, but as we mature and develop and move out into adult life, this desire for parental approval ideally should come to an end. This moment in life is usually referred to as cutting the psychological cord with our parents. When this occurs, we have become an adult, psychologically speaking; individuation has occurred, to use psychological jargon. This process does not occur at a defined age; its timing is different for each family and individual, but ideally, it happens sometime in the early twenties.

Peers

Besides our parents having a tremendous influence on our self-esteem, our peer group can also affect our self-esteem. My mother used to tell me that I was so handsome and good-looking in her attempt to build my self-esteem and confidence regarding girls when I was in high school. When I went to school and was with my peers, my experience was totally the opposite of what my mother was telling me. She tried to build me up, but my comeback to her was, "If I am so good-looking, Mom, why doesn't the homecoming queen want to go out on a date with me?" So even though my parents tried to validate my self-esteem, I gave my peer group the power to take it away.

Wanting to be accepted by our peer group is a very powerful psychological force during our childhood development process. Our acceptance by our peer group can start as early as elementary school and becomes an even greater force in middle school, and then becomes a full-blown force by high school. If we stay with the same peer group from one school to another and don't move away, we can become psychologically locked in by the same peers from elementary school through high school—and perhaps college as well if we stay in the same geographic area. If we get positive validation by your peers, then this continuity from one school level to another can be a comforting feeling; but if you are judged in a negative way, this peer entrapment can be stifling. Once your peers label you, you become stuck with that label—it's an identity that is hard to change.

Being part of a group in high school is important to having a sense of identity. Being part of the "right" group can affect your self-esteem; it can open doors for you in a social way. When you are a young adolescent, your peer group can provide you with a sense of security that you may not have anywhere else in your life. This is why peer conformity and group acceptance is such a powerful force that can transcend parental validation.

The standards or attributes that determine self-esteem in middle and high school can remain into adult life, even if they are no longer relevant. Some people never get out of high school psychologically. They are still living and judging themselves by high-school values even though they might be 35 years old. This is particularly true for those who never leave their hometown. The judgments and criticism made by your peers can last a lifetime if you don't deal with them in a constructive manner. Things that insecure boys said to me in the high school locker room were extremely painful and vicious at the time. I allowed them to destroy certain aspects of my self-esteem. Those judgments would still be operating on my self-esteem if I didn't confront them as an adult and see how ridiculous they were in retrospect.

I remember how both the boys and girls labeled certain girls as "whores." These girls had their own peer group and hung out together at school. Looking back, I am sure they weren't prostitutes, but they got this label probably because they were more sexually mature and active than all the sexually insecure boys and girls who were making this judgment at the time. My concern in looking back is what negative effect these judgments had on those girls in their adult life. I sometimes wonder if these judgments scarred them for life. There were other peer groups too, such as the jocks, the stoners, and the greasers. All of them had their own identity and certain requirements to be a part of the group.

When I was in high school in the late 1960s, there were certain things, activities, or associations that gave a high school male self-esteem among his peers. One of those things was having a car, and especially a car that was customized into something unique—a hot rod. If you had what was considered a cool car, then just by owning this automobile you were considered a cool guy. Being the cool guy meant that you had a lot of friends who wanted to hang out with you, and most importantly, wanted to ride around in your car so they could feel cool as well. Owning the hot car also acted as a "babe magnet." The girls wanted to ride in the cool car because it made them feel worthy by being seen in a hot car.

Everyone connected to the hot car either by owning the car or by just being a passenger would garner some kind of self-esteem. This type of self-esteem is acquired by an external possession, which is a very tenuous way to define an individual's self-worth.

Besides the type of car a person had in high school, another thing that made you a worthwhile individual was if you played a varsity sport. Not every sport was considered cool; it was only football, baseball, or basketball. As a male, if you wore a letterman's jacket or sweater around campus, you held your head high and your chest out, because you were a varsity athlete and everyone was somewhat in awe. I am not sure if this tradition still goes on at high school campuses today, but it was very common back in my day. Again, an individual's self-esteem is defined by something externally, by playing an athletic sport. Instead of self-esteem being affected by an object, like a car, it's defined by performing an activity.

Other males wanted to be friends with these athletes because they could vicariously feel good about themselves as a friend of a high school celebrity. Athletes were the stars of the school, and who doesn't want to be a part of a star's entourage? The girls flocked to them. They had no problem getting a date for Saturday night. Their sexuality was being affirmed by what they did, and not who they were as individuals. What they were like as people didn't seem to matter; they were the stars in this closed world of high school. For many of these athletes this star mentally continued into college, and even into professional sports if that's where they ended up.

The last criteria that could determine a male's self-esteem in high school was what social group he associated with. Being a part of the "club" gave a boy a sense of worth. These weren't gangs as we know them today, but I am sure they give men that same sense of worth as the quasi-fraternities did back in high school. Each club had their turf around school where they would congregate at lunchtime. Each club had its image or characteristics that defined its identity as well as its members. Some clubs were focused around athletics, "the jocks," or the "bad boys" who got into fights and started trouble. These clubs gave their members a sense of meaning and identity during the turbulent adolescent years of high school.

So the type of car you owned, what sport you played, what group of friends you had played a significant role in affecting a boy's self-esteem in high school. I am sure these same factors play a role with male high school students today as they did back in the 1960s.

When I was in high school, I struck out on all counts. I didn't have a car of my own—my mother thought car ownership would affect my motivation to do my homework. So I rode my bike to and from school or I walked. I rode my bike part way to school until I met up with my other friends who didn't have a car at their disposal. We didn't want to be seen by our other peers because this would give them ammunition to make fun of us later, once we were at school. It just wasn't cool to ride your bike to school. It was considered very geeky.

The next benchmark of self-esteem was playing a cool varsity sport. I did play a varsity sport for all my high school years, but it wasn't one of the right sports—it was just tennis. I played tennis as a means to escape regular physical education, which I hated at the time. Tennis was not as popular then as it later became. It was considered a "sissy sport," not macho like football or basketball. The baseball team would make fun of us when my tennis team would get on the bus to go to the same school for a match. I had a letterman's jacket, but the wrong sport. In hindsight I am glad I played tennis, because I still play— tennis is for life, and those other sports are difficult to play later in life.

I struck out on having a car, and I didn't play the right sport, so the only thing to save my self-esteem was belonging to a socially accepted peer clique on campus. I flunked this benchmark as well. My peer clique at high school was what I called the "insecure boys club." We didn't congregate in the quad area, but away from everyone at lunchtime. We gave ourselves support, but not self-esteem, by hanging out with each other.

As a result of not reaching any of the standards for self-esteem in high school, I had poor self-esteem and zero confidence within the social structure and the whole dating scene. I studied, played tennis, and hung out with my friends. In hindsight, I guess this wasn't such a bad thing, considering the trouble I could have gotten into at the time. It's hard to change your self-esteem and self-identity when you go through middle school and high school with the same people. You get locked into a certain image, and that's the way people relate to you socially. If you move to different geographical areas, it's easier to change. For me this change didn't happen until I went to the University of California at Berkeley.

When I went to Cal as an undergrad, I lived in a coed dorm where no one really knew each other. I had a clean slate, no baggage from the past except for my suitcase of clothes. A chance to start over and break free from my life in high school and my home town of Long Beach, California. What I began to notice right away was that very few people had cars and the students who did had beat up VW bugs or vans. The students weren't impressed by cars. In fact, a car was an irritant, because there was very little parking available. These were the days of anti-materialism, and cars were seen as a necessary evil, not something to celebrate. So unlike high school, having a car at college didn't make a person cool.

The other aspect that was different from high school was that there wasn't a social clique system. People in the fraternities and sororities were a small minority at that time. Students who belonged to these "houses" were not seen as hip or cool; in fact, they were looked upon as being anachronistic. As for the rest of us, we were all the same, one big group— Cal students. So when I moved into my dorm not knowing anyone else, I felt comfortable right away. I could walk right up to anyone, male or female, and there wasn't any judgment that I wasn't in the right social group. This experience was incredibly liberating. I started to feel like I wasn't such a bad, socially inept individual. Girls wouldn't reject me because I wasn't a member of the right social group; we were all in the same boat.

The last major difference in attitude was that playing a varsity sport didn't carry the same social significance that it did in high school. Within the "jock culture", there was a great deal of admiration for being a star athlete, but this recognition didn't transcend within the general campus population. In fact, athletes were not seen as a big deal as they were in the past or as they are now.

When I got to Cal, everything that made a male feel good about himself in high school—cars, clubs, and sports—didn't hold the same value. In fact, they held very little value. What was important was being a "freak." Long hair, radical politics, and the arts—especially current rock and roll music—were the things that made a person hip or cool. The whole "Woodstock Nation" was in full force on the Cal campus and many other universities and colleges at that time. I was able to fit into this scene and, low and behold, my self-esteem and self-confidence increased dramatically. The majority of people I encountered accepted me, which was a very different experience than when I was in high school.

So in one location, high school, Long Beach, California, I didn't feel good about myself, and when I moved away four hundred miles north to Berkeley, California, I become a completely different person, and my self-esteem in general increased. What's up with this experience? I am sure that I am not the only one who experienced this phenomenon.

At that time, I realized something important: how much power I gave my peer group to determine my self-esteem. You would think that this awareness would be obvious to me at that time, but it wasn't. Worrying about what the peer group thought was so much a part of the culture that it was just what you did at that time. I had to remove myself from that particular peer group to see what I was doing. When this insight hit me, I reacted by getting angry with myself for being such a wimp. This of course was a mistake, because it's not a good idea to get angry with yourself when you have fear, because it makes the fear increase. I will discuss this concept in further detail. I took the power away from my high school peers and realized that they were not the masters of my self-esteem; I recognized that I am the only one who can determine my worth. So I took the power back. This step was similar to cutting the cord with my parents.

When I went to my first ten-year high school reunion, it was such a pleasure, because I wasn't anxious and afraid of my fellow classmates. They were just peers of the same graduating class; in other words, we were all on the same plane. No one was better, superior, smarter, or better-looking; we all had something that we brought to the party that made us special. I could go right up to the high school homecoming queen, say hi, and introduce myself, something I wouldn't have dreamed of doing ten years earlier. She was just another woman in the room, and she had changed as well. Her appearance wasn't the same. She had aged, as we all had, but she was still someone I wanted to talk to and break free of my past fears of rejection and insecurity. I was a much more confident person who was beginning to love himself.

For many people the pattern of giving our peer group culture the power to determine our self-esteem continues into our adult life. The whole notion of "keeping up with the Joneses" abounds throughout suburbia. Owning an expensive car or a big their house in a good neighborhood can be seen as ways to validate someone's self-esteem. Not that having nice cars or homes isn't a pleasant quality of life issue, they just can't be seen as giving someone self-esteem. All of these material things are superficial window dressing that really aren't about the person. It's just exterior packaging that loses its value over time. The problem also is that there is always someone with a bigger house around the corner or a nicer car, so this type of peer validation through material items is a bottomless pit when it comes to defining your individual worth. You never really get self-esteem this way—it's fleeting.

When we look to our peers for self-validation, they will generally base their assessment of us on our performance in some area. In high school, being the homecoming queen, the student body president, the football quarterback, or the class clown drew attention by validating these individuals' self-esteem. I don't want to imply that performing some type of activity well is not a healthy goal, but where the problem lies is that we can't put all our self-worth solely on what we do or how we perform. So many examples of this pattern occur in our daily life.

What happens to people who base their whole self-identity and self-esteem on what they do and not who they are as individuals with specific traits that give them worth? There is no problem for them until they are no longer able to perform at the same level when they were validated, or when they're not able to do the activity at all. I remember seeing the popular student body president from my high school at Cal, but at college, he was just a small fish in a big pond. He couldn't handle this change, and fell off the deep end psychologically.

In my private practice, I have seen many men and women who are no longer able to perform their jobs for some reason. Whether it's being an attorney, mother, stockbroker, or athlete, when they can no longer perform their career, they fall into a depression. This is because they no longer know who they are; they have lost their sense of identity. They had all their eggs in one basket in terms of their psychological identity, which was based on their ability to perform their roles. I try to help them out of their identity crisis by helping them realize that there are other roles or identities that are very important in their lives. I want them to realize that they possess valuable personal qualities that haven't gone away just because they can't perform a particular task.

Having your self-esteem validated by performance is scary because most people don't always perform well all the time. If you're having a bad day performing or someone attacks your performance, does your self-esteem go down? Your self-esteem will go up and down like a roller coaster when performance is the sole determinate. I love public speaking; but if I let my self-esteem and self–confidence be defined only by my speaking performance, I would be terrified, and would probably develop a great deal of speaking anxiety and perform badly. I always have to remember that I am not what I do. If someone is critical of my performance, they are not being critical of me personally. As a speaker or a therapist, I need to keep reminding myself of this fact. Sometimes the content of the material or my position can threaten people, and they will attack me personally, but the truth is they don't really know "me"—they only know what I represent to them. Sometimes it goes the other way when they praise me as a speaker or a therapist, which is always a positive experience; but again, it's not me they are praising, it's Dan the therapist or teacher; they don't really know me as a person. My wife knows the real Dan, separate from all the roles I might play.

Opposite or Same Sex

When it comes to giving our power away regarding our self-esteem, the lovers in our life can have an incredible impact. This process starts when our attention turns to wanting the acceptance of a girl or boy. Generally, this need for acceptance occurs sometime in earlier adolescence, at twelve or thirteen, and sometimes even earlier. It happens at that first dance situation where the boys and girls all bunch up into their groups and stare at each other. The boys trying to act cool, but inside they are nervous because they know that they have to make that first move and ask a girl if she wants to dance and risk hearing the big NO. The girls stand around waiting to be asked to dance with one of the cute boys. If they're not asked to dance, then their self-esteem is going to take a hit. My own girls used to count the number of times they were asked to dance. They kept score as if the more they were asked to dance, the better they felt about themselves. Of course, the reverse was true. Those early school dances were proving grounds for an individual's self-esteem in relation to the opposite sex. Anxiety levels were high given what was at stake psychologically. The effects of these early experiences with the opposite sex could have a long-lasting impact on a person well into their adult life.

The Self-Esteem Guillotine

In my day, the critical rite of passage was asking a girl out on a date. It was a pretty formal process with rules of conduct. One rule was that you needed to make the phone call by Wednesday for a weekend date. If there was a girl I was interested in asking out, I would do some scouting with my friends or her friends to see if anyone might know if she liked me in any way. Having this advance information made the phone call a whole lot less risky. What was the risk? The big fear of the experience of sexual rejection and its associated pain. Getting the girl's phone number was a major task, because the only resource was the phone book. Then the moment arrived when it was time to make the call to her house. Making this phone call was like putting my head in a self-esteem guillotine and I felt as though I was handing the girl the rope that possibly could release the blade that would cut off my head.

It was all based on her response to my question of whether she would go to a movie or not. My anxiety levels were off the chart, because I was giving this girl the power to decide my worth as a male. If she said yes to my request, I was spared the blade and my self-worth was saved, but if her answer was no, I was rolling on the floor in agony. My mother never had to asked, "So what did she say about going out with you?" She could tell by my reaction and behavior. If the girl said yes then I was jumping up and down, and I was Mr. Happy to everyone in my family. If she said no, then I was slamming doors and telling everyone to leave me alone.

I am sure many of you can relate to this experience at some time in your life. What the "no" meant to my desire to go out with her was that I was rejected—I was no good, ugly, not cool—all of my insecurities at that time came raging to the psychological surface. Most adolescents are very insecure about their sexuality. Perceived rejection can have a major negative impact on an adolescent's self-esteem. Maybe the girl wasn't allowed by her parents to date anyone at that time. I assumed it was all about me and my inadequacies. I didn't want to ask the question—"Why won't you go out with me?" That would be too awkward for everyone involved.

The process of giving women the power to determine my self-esteem continued all through high school and college, until I was in my mid-twenties. For some people, it continues through adult life and even into the marital bedroom. I was able to break out of giving women the power when I started to realize that what I thought was rejection wasn't really rejection at all.

This realization occurred when I was single and would frequent the singles bars in the 1970s. By this time in my life, my self-esteem in general was fairly high compared to where it had been. Generally, when I went out to the "singles scene," I usually had some kind of an agenda. I wanted something: to dance with a girl to get her phone number. I might even want to have sex with her, to have a relationship of some kind. When I went up to a woman and express one of these desires and she said no thanks, was that rejection? Normally, I would perceive the situation as a rejection, and I would react emotionally by being hurt, because I was taking this rejection personally just like I did when I was kid. This time, I analyzed the situation and how I felt because as a young therapist, that's what I did, and I had a major realization. I wanted to tell those women who said "no" to my desire to come back—I wanted to tell them I wasn't such a bad guy; I had attributes they were missing out on if they were to reject me. I had never felt this way in the past. My previous attitude was that I was lucky to have a girl who was interested in being involved with me. At this point in my life, my thinking changed, and I had a sense that I was bringing something to the party if the woman wanted to stick around and find out what qualities existed.

Then the epiphany hit me: how could a woman I had never met before really reject me? She may not like my appearance, or have any sexual chemistry with me, but is this rejection? The answer is a big NO. She can't really reject me when she has no clue as to my values, personality, or interests. She hasn't gotten to know me other than what she sees on the outside, which is just packaging. So if I am not being rejected, then what is really going on? Because it doesn't feel that pleasant to be told no to my desires.

When an individual asserts some type of personal desire that is not met, they are not being rejected personally, but instead they are being disappointed. When I asked those women in the singles bars for their phone numbers, or if they wanted to dance with me, and they said no, they were not giving me what I wanted, but they weren't rejecting me personally. You don't always get what you want in the adult world, which may not make you happy, but you aren't being rejected as a person just because someone says no to your advances. Rejection is very painful and can be devastating to a person's self-esteem. To reject someone, you need to spend some time with them and to know their values, interests, their background, and what their personality is like. All this takes time, and in today's dating world, interactions happen so fast and so superficially that it would be hard to really reject someone.

When I realized that most likely I was being disappointed rather than rejected when I made a "cold call" to a woman, I was set free from the experience of the self-esteem guillotine. I wish now that I had this insight when I was back in high school; what a difference it could have made. The fear of rejection inhibits so many people from taking personal risks, keeping them trapped in boring, rutted patterns. The fear of rejection even transcends into a marital relationship where you think it wouldn't occur, but it does, even with people who profess their love and acceptance for each other. Rejection takes place in long-term relationships, because people can change radically over time, and the person who you married in your late twenties may be very different when you reach late forties, and by then you may want nothing to do with them. So the next time you assert yourself with the opposite sex, and they say no to what you want, ask yourself: are you being rejected or are they just disappointing your desire?

Breaking Up Is Hard to Do

When a relationship ends, it's not uncommon for the one who doesn't want to dissolve the relationship to take the loss personally and feel rejected. "What's wrong with me that he or she doesn't want to be with me," they ask. Is it that I'm too fat, not fun enough, that I didn't want to have sex very often, or that I yelled too much? What do I need to change about myself? The partner who is left behind focuses on all their insecurities, thinking that these are the reasons their partner is leaving them.

If their partner is having an affair, they may believe the other woman or man must have something that they don't, and that's why their spouse went outside their marriage to the other person. Generally, their self-esteem is in the gutter as a result of the affair. In all my experience as a therapist dealing with the extramarital affair situation, it has little to do with the fact that one partner was lacking a personal quality. It's more related to the lack of emotional intimacy within the relationship.

Why do people who are in a break-up situation in a relationship immediately believe it's all about them? There could be all kinds of other issues that have nothing to do with any of their shortcomings. They assume it's about them because then they feel that they have control to make the situation different. They think they can make changes so they can get their partner back. It gives them a false sense of control, of keeping the relationship together. People generally don't like to face the fact that they are vulnerable and don't have control over certain situations and people.

Sometimes they can make changes that allow the couple to reconcile. One example is if I am providing therapy to an alcoholic, and their drinking is the reason their spouse doesn't want to continue the relationship unless their alcoholic spouse follows a path to recovery. If the alcoholic spouse works through a program and becomes sober, then relationship reconciliation is possible.

Often in a relationship breakup or dissolution, the partner who wants to stay together believes that they have failed in keeping their relationship together. Again, they are working under the assumption that they somehow had control in the first place and that they failed at maintaining control. Sometimes I hear comments like: "What's wrong with you? You couldn't keep your partner so they had to go somewhere else for their happiness." This attitude implies that we have control over our lover's happiness and that we have failed if our partner leaves us for someone else. You would never want control over an adult in an intimate relationship, because the control will destroy the intimacy. We are not responsible for another adult's happiness in this lifetime. This belief is the ticket to co-dependency. How can you fail when you didn't have control in the first place? Unfortunately, the individual who gets "dumped" by their lover often believes they failed. They feel inadequate in having successful intimate relationships and that there is something inherently wrong with them; as a result, they have deflated self-esteem regarding their relationships.

One major way we give the opposite sex the power to determine our self-esteem is in the area of appearance: how we look; what we wear; how our body looks; the style of our hair; the constant focus on our "superficial packaging." The entire plastic surgery business is a major beneficiary of this concern. Don't get me wrong; I think it's great to try to look your best and to feel good about your appearance. Where it crosses the line into psychological dysfunction is when we connect self-esteem to our appearance, and we look for the approval of what others think, especially lovers, to determine our appeal or worth. What happens when a person looks externally to others or to one man or woman is that you give our power away and then you start to lose your sense of self.

Here's an example: Jane is dating Bill, who likes women with blonde hair, but Jane happens to be brunette, so she changes her hair color to please him. Then she finds out that he likes women with large breasts. So to keep Bill interested and sexually turned on to her she decides to make an appointment with a plastic surgeon to have her breasts augmented. So now Jane is blonde, with large breasts, and feels pretty good about herself because she thinks Bill loves her. The question is does he love her for who she is or what the packaging looks like? Jane doesn't want to ask that question because it's too upsetting. Their relationship continues for about six months, but Jane starts noticing that Bill is not as interested in spending time together, and she is starting to feel more and more insecure around him. Finally, she confronts him about his interest in another woman and he confesses that he is seeing someone else, Sue, [who is Japanese,] and he finds her very exciting.

To say the least Jane is devastated, incredibly hurt, and angry that after all she did to herself that Bill leaves her for someone else. She no longer knows who she is and feels rejected. Two weeks later, she meets a new guy, John, and he is excited to spend time with her, and she suddenly feels better about herself. This pattern is called the roller coaster of self-esteem. Jane is emotionally going up and down along with her self-esteem. She might want to medicate the ride with alcohol or anti-depressants to numb the pain, but she is what therapists call treating the symptoms and not really getting at the core problem. The core issue is that she is giving the power to men to determine her worth. She doesn't realize that their evaluation of her is based on superficial packaging.

If men or women put their self-esteem in this area of evaluation, they are entering the world of insecurity and powerlessness, and the feeling of being the victim of men or women. Whenever we give the power away to another adult for anything, it will breed contempt and resentment for that person and the relationship itself. It's a no-win situation.

Sometimes in marital relationships, it feels like one of the spouses needs the other to constantly give them compliments about how they look. It seems as if they are a bottomless pit for compliments or validation. The reason for this is that their spouse has no internal self-esteem regarding their appearance, so if they are not getting positive feedback they go into a panic. This puts a great deal of pressure on one spouse to be responsible for their lover's self-worth, which they will begin to resent and will withhold feedback. It's a wonderful gift to give compliments, but to be responsible again for an adult's self-esteem is a whole other story.

This need for external validation from a spouse or girl/boy friend is intensified when an individual wasn't validated or accepted by their parents, especially the opposite sex parent. They have a void in their self-esteem, and they want their significant other to fill the void. This gives their significant other way too much power to determine their self-esteem. This won't work and will kill the intimacy within the relationship. No one can fill your self-esteem void but yourself.

THE MEDIA

The media impact on people's self-esteem is pervasive. Television, the Internet, the motion picture industry, the music industry, all forms of advertising including magazines, billboards, radio, all impact people's daily lives directly or in an unconscious way. Unless someone lives in the wild, they are exposed to the media blitz all the time starting at a very young age.

We as a culture are exposed to so many visual images through the different channels of the media that it's hard to escape. The problem with these images is that they set a benchmark of the ideal look for masculinity and femininity. These images gradually become a part of our consciousness, and we compare ourselves to them. These images aren't real; they are doctored in all kinds of ways to create the illusion of perfection. The problem is that humans aren't perfect; we have flaws and imperfections and we age. It's all beyond our control no matter how many plastic surgeries we might have in our lifetime. So when we make the comparison between what we see in our own mirror and what we see in the media, we as a culture are going to feel inadequate, not good enough, always falling short. As a result of this belief of inadequacy, our self-esteem plummets in the area of sexuality and body image. Our sense of being a man or a woman takes a major hit on a daily basis. Much of this process can occur at a subliminal level without an individual knowing that it's going on within their psyche. This covert process is what makes the effect of the media so devious.

Why would the media want to destroy people's self-esteem? The media is an extension of the advertising industry, whose purpose it is to get consumers to buy things. So the real culprit here is the business world that wants to make money giving people the opportunity to buy products to "help fix" the consumer's self-esteem problem that the business world helped to create in a way. As consumers, all we have to do is buy the right product and then we can be perfect and stay forever young. This is at the heart of the message that the advertising industry bombards us with. The problem is that no matter how many things we buy, we can't fix "the problem." We just wonder what's wrong with us that this stuff doesn't work. We personalize the issue and think that we just don't have the right product; and we need to keep looking and buying.

When we can decode this media message, that buying a certain product will fix our self-esteem, and replace it with the attitude that these products are an "ad-on," or enhancement, and not the real fix, then we will no longer make purchases driven by our own insecurities. Of course, the makeup and plastic surgery business won't be too happy if we make this change in attitude. This is just one example of how the advertising industry embeds messages connected to buying products.

Other messages about our sexuality are connected to certain products. If you buy this cologne, drink this beer, or own this car, then women or men are going to want to be with you in a sexual way. Now, generally, they don't just come out and say this in their advertising, but they imply it through the use of images.

The psychological issue occurs when we buy the specific product and don't get the woman or man as like the ad tells us. We still find ourselves alone without a partner. As a result, we feel frustrated and angry because what we thought would happen didn't, and our expectations aren't fulfilled. Not only do we have an emotional reaction, but also we start to think that there is something wrong with us. We personalize the fact that we don't get what the ad in some way promises. Again we our getting set up with false expectations by the advertising media. None of this process is going on at a conscious level, because if it were, we would reject the concept outright.

The major change in the advertising industry and our culture is that the images and embedded messages are being exposed to younger and younger children. Children don't have the ability to differentiate between the reality of the images they see on television, the Internet, billboards, or magazines, and real life. The embedded messages are established early in an individual's development, and by the time they became an adult—and might have some ability to reject them on a conscious level—they are already there on a subconscious level doing their psychological damage.

This is an example of how the use of media images in pornography adversely affects men's self-perception of their sexual anatomy. Women's bodies get distorted in pornography, but this also happens to men. How do most males learn about the size of the penis? When they are going through puberty, they don't look at other boys' genitals in the locker room during gym class. If they got caught looking, they would be opening the door to attack for a variety of reasons. When they are in the men's restroom, they are not checking out what other men's genitals look like while urinating. So most boys live in a vacuum when it comes to knowing the normal size of a penis.

For many teenage boys, pornography is very accessible through the Internet. Unfortunately, the explicit images that they see set the standards for their expectations of what sex is all about without much relationship to reality. When it comes to anatomy, what porn producers do is to search the countryside for the anatomical "freaks." Large or even gigantic is what they are looking for in male genitals, the genetic aberration. This is the type of male they use in their adult videos and pictures. Along comes an immature, insecure, curious teenage boy and he looks at these images and then compares himself to the men in the images and feels more inadequate and insecure about the size of his penis. Then there are those who play on this insecurity by selling products that they say can fix this problem. In reality, though, there is nothing other than some type of medical procedure that can increase penis size. Women have a similar issue in this culture regarding breast size.

The media is an all-powerful force that affects us on an everyday basis. The images the media uses to sell products generally are images of perfection. The problem is that perfection doesn't exist, but we as a culture start to believe the embedded message that we can be perfect—all we have to do is try and get the right product. The other related message is that without being perfect we won't be loved, and that we won't or can't be beautiful or attractive. The truth is that perfection exists in fantasyland, and once a person understands this reality, they set themselves free from this set up for inadequacy and low self-esteem.

You Are Not a Victim of All These Influences

Now that I have addressed the major influences that can impact our self-esteem, I don't want to imply that we are just victims of these influences, and that there is nothing we can do about their effect. (There are other influences that I haven't addressed here, but I believe these are the major ones.) Once a person becomes aware of how the media, peers, parents, and lovers have affected their self-esteem, they can make attitude changes to lessen their influence. If you have given your power away to these influences without knowing it, then you can get your power back once you see and understand the process. It requires a heightened sense of awareness of how we can so easily give our power away.

The Pursuit of Perfection

One common attitude or belief that impacts so many people—whether it comes from their parents, lovers, or the media—is the concept of perfection. Some people even label themselves as being perfectionists. The problem with this label and belief is that human beings are not perfect. We have flaws, we make mistakes, we forget, and we age, all of which affect our functioning. If an individual bases their self-worth on attaining perfection, then they are setting themselves up for poor self-esteem or self-image. This is such a common problem in the area of self-esteem development. So many people tear themselves down because they expect perfection or project that others expect perfection. Having a perfectionist attitude falls into what I will later address as a cognitive distortion.

In western culture, where perfectionism really takes its toll is on women's self-esteem regarding their body image. As I stated earlier, the media only exposes images of women that have been doctored to achieve the look of perfection. No wrinkles, no fat, no stretch marks, no blemishes, not even any pores—just perfection, flawless beauty. These standards of impossibility don't exist in the real world of human beings. Is it any wonder that women have trouble feeling good about their own bodies? When I listen to women receive compliments about their looks or body, they tend to discount the compliment with a "yeah, but I am a little too big here, or I am too small here, or I have this mark here." Because they aren't perfect physically they can't even hear the compliment. As my fellow therapist, Sheilah Fish, used to say, "They focus on the hole of the donut as opposed to the donut itself."

Men can also participate in this same kind of body loathing, but mostly you hear it from women, because they are under the constant scrutiny from others or themselves regarding their bodies. Their sexuality, lovability, and self-esteem are always on the line regarding their looks. It's no wonder that many just give up the pursuit and let themselves go regarding their physical appearance just to get out from under the pressure of achieving perfection. They may be out from under the pressure, but their self-judgment continues nonetheless, which will continue to take a psychological toll in other ways, such as through depression, eating disorders, or substance abuse. Women who seek perfection and buy into the social definition of what is beautiful will be trapped in a no-win situation regarding their physical appearance.

Another area where the expectation for perfection takes a toll on our self-esteem is when we are trying to develop new behaviors or tasks.

People who have to be perfect have real trouble doing something new, because in their mind they have to do the new activity perfectly, right out of the starting gate. There is no learning curve for this type of individual; they don't give themselves a break for being new at something. Either they do it perfectly right away or they don't do it all, which means that most likely they won't take on anything new.

As a result, individuals who expect perfection in themselves tend to have a very difficult time growing into new areas of life, and they tend to get stuck in the same old thing. They can't develop self-confidence because they don't allow themselves to make mistakes with repeated experiences. This process was clearly demonstrated to me by my two daughters when I took them skiing.

At a young age, my daughter, Danielle, would attack the ski hill without much fear of falling, and when she did, she would just laugh it off, get up, and continue down the hill. No problem. Her sister, Michelle, on the other hand, who was a year younger, was a whole different story. She approached the hill with much more trepidation. When she fell, she would get incredibly upset with herself and the situation. She was so embarrassed that she fell, because she thought that everyone on the hill was looking at her and passing judgment. If she made a mistake, "Oh my god," it was a major catastrophe, and no matter what I would tell her, it didn't change her emotions. She was going to be upset and that was that, end of story. She would often just quit and go back to the ski lodge until she cooled down and tried again. At that time, Michelle was a perfectionist about whatever she did, and this kept her from making mistakes and allowing for a learning curve. Consequently, Michelle never developed much confidence as a skier and never progressed passed the "bunny hill" level of ability. However, her sister, Danielle, was able to develop a great deal of confidence ski-ing and became an advance skier as an adult. Danielle was able to take the risk of making a mistake, which allowed her to grow in confidence as compared to Michelle. What's ironic is that in some ways they have reversed roles in some areas of their lives as they have gotten older.

When we can risk making mistakes and not being perfect, we can try out new activities that make us more interesting and less bored with ourselves. We don't stay stuck in the same ruts doing the same old thing. We are able to venture out of our usual comfort zones. Bob Dylan's song lyric, "He who isn't being born, is busy dying has always stuck with me as a mantra for living." In other words if you're not busy taking risks doing new activities and experiences, you're no longer living and growing; you're just waiting to die. It's a powerful message for those who want fulfillment in their lives.

One day I realized that I have been doing the same sports activities for most of my adult life—tennis and skiing. That's all I did, and I was pretty good and proficient at both, but for a long time, I never did anything different or new. Maybe I was getting a little bored with myself. So in the spirit of the Dylan song I said to myself, "Try something new; go for it Dan—take a risk.

The activity I picked was wind surfing. This was a new experience for me, so I thought it might be a good idea if I took some lessons, so I went to the local lake and gave it a try. I got out there on the board after I took my lessons, and I kept falling down with everyone on the shore watching me, including my wife. At that point, I could have felt ashamed and embarrassed that I wasn't doing it right, or I could have just laughed and enjoyed the fact that I was doing something new and refreshing out of my usual comfort zone. I chose the latter and had fun, and eventually began to stay on the board and enjoy the experience. At that point, I had a new activity to enjoy and make my life richer and something I could talk about and share with another person. Once I was able to break out of the perfectionist trap I was in, I was able to add something new to my sense of self-identity and expand my sense of self, which all contribute to improved self-esteem. Self-esteem improves because with new aspects to my identity, I bring more to a relationship or even more to the party. Because of all this improvement, my social self-confidence is greatly heightened as well.

Take the risk and break out of your comfort zone of the "same old, same old," and as the Nike slogan says, "Just Do It."

When Achievement Becomes a Problem

Another destructive attitude that can destroy an individual's self-esteem is the belief that a person is only as good as what they have produced, accomplished, or achieved, in the moment or in their lifetime. For them, it isn't about what kind of person they are, but what they have achieved. This attitude weighs especially heavy with men, although it can affect women as well.

The psychologist, Bernie Zilbergeld, who wrote the book, *Male Sexuality*, stated that the three A's of manhood are achieve, achieve, achieve. If a man isn't achieving something or producing something, then he is just a "bum," worthless and no good. The man who isn't achieving has self-esteem that's in the toilet.

Some people live with the pressure that they are only as good as their last performance. This attitude creates so much anxiety that it can cripple someone from taking on any performance because his or her self-worth is always on the line. I see this performance anxiety with students who have to take a test, attorneys in a trial situation, public speakers giving a presentation, or men who are insecure about their ability to get an erection.

To put your self-esteem in the area of performance or achievement is a setup for psychological and physical disaster. It keeps you from enjoying life. It inhibits so many men from enjoying the world of pleasure. Women generally don't receive the message that relaxing and receiving pleasure for pleasure's sake is a bad thing, a total waste of time as men do in our culture.

I remember well how hard it was for me to just sit on the beach for several hours and relax and enjoy the whole experience of being in such a beautiful setting. I would sit there thinking, "Now, what I am creating, what I am producing, what do I have to show for the time spent on the beach?" My wife could justify her time because for her it was all about getting a tan. I wasn't into getting a tan because I would always burn, so that couldn't be my goal at the beach. This was before we knew about the connection between sunbathing early on and the occurrence of skin cancer later in life. If there were waves and the water was warm enough, I could go swimming or boogie boarding, and then I could justify being at the beach, because I was doing something and not just sitting on the beach being bored. The problem for me was that most of the time I went to the beach in Northern California where the water was freezing and not conducive to swimming, but the beach was naturally beautiful. Something had to change, and that was my attitude.

My attitude changed with the realization that I really wasn't wasting time just sitting on the beach, but instead I was relaxing and recharging myself, taking the experience in through my senses: sight, smell, sound, touch, and taste. What I was taking in was the experience of *pleasure*. Wow, what a concept. I didn't have to work and produce and achieve something that would only drain me, but instead I could take in the pleasure of the experience and re-energize myself. I experienced the concept of just *being* as opposed to *doing* something all the time. I was able to give myself permission to relax and not feel guilty. By allowing myself to experience and create this type of pleasure without guilt was a very loving gift I was giving to myself. I was taking care of myself in a very different way; I was nurturing myself and developing the confidence that I could take care of myself without depending on a woman to nurture me.

Once I could make this attitude shift from always having to do something as opposed to being involved in the experience, I could apply this attitude to many other situations in my life. I don't know how many skiing experiences I ruined because I always felt I had to conquer a bigger mountain or a harder ski run. I couldn't just enjoy the moment of being on the mountain. I believed that I had to progress and achieve greater accomplishments, and I pushed everyone I was with in the same way. It wasn't fun for anyone, and conflicts and fights would occur, so the ski trip wasn't that relaxing for anyone.

In my clinical practice, I ask my male clients a simple question when I first start seeing them: "When you aren't working at your job, what do you do for fun?" Usually their answers go like this:

- "Well, I like to work out in the gym."

- "I like to work on my house."
- "I usually work on my car."
- "I work on my golf game."

The operative word here is work. These male clients have to be doing something; they just can't be, and have fun and pleasure unless they are in some altered mental state. I guess their drug of choice shuts off that voice in their head that they should be accomplishing something, and that pleasure is a waste of their time.

We all have heard the saying, "All work and no play makes Jack a dull boy." I think that says it all, only Jack is no longer a boy but a man, and he represents so many men out there. All work and no play or pleasure equates with a lot of angry men who are burned out on their lives and their relationships because they block the anger and as a result find themselves in various degrees of depression. This pattern is true for women as well. Besides depression, the stress of holding back the anger has a negative effect on them physically as well. Their immune system is compromised, and this in turn makes them vulnerable to disease, which may have something to do with why men die before their time relative to women.

Being able to give yourself pleasure and to allow pleasure into your life is one major practical step toward learning to love yourself. Being able to give yourself pleasure is a wonderful gift to yourself. When you can give and create pleasure in your life then it is so easy to give to your significant others. We get the cultural message that giving yourself pleasure is selfish, a negative thing, and if you do it, you should feel guilty; so many people in America have this belief, which gets in the way of their ability to enjoy themselves. They often have to use alcohol or drugs to escape this self-criticism to enjoy the pleasure of the moment without guilt. It's okay to work, but to create and enjoy pleasure can be viewed as a sin of some kind, and seems to go back to our Puritan heritage.

Chapter Six

Creating Your Own Self-Esteem

N ow that I have discussed the influences and difficulties with developing any positive self-esteem in this culture, I want to talk about how an individual develops self-esteem without giving their power away to other sources. How does a person develop what I call their core sense of self-esteem? I want them to have self-esteem that does not immediately change because of external factors.

The direct approach I use in helping a client develop or build their self-esteem is to have them pick the part of their self-identity where they believe they have low self-esteem. The process of creating positive self-esteem is the same regardless of what part of their identity they choose. One common area of low self-esteem is an individual's sense of being a lover/sexuality. They may believe that they aren't a good lover sexually or that there is something wrong with them because their spouse left them for someone else. As a result, their self-esteem in this area is in the gutter.

After we establish the part of their self-identity where they want better self-esteem, I have them write down the positive attributes they believe they possess that relate to that particular area of self. If they have concerns about being a lover, I have them list the qualities that they think make them a good lover—not what others think or say, but what they believe. If the client isn't sure of what qualities they have, I ask them what they think are the qualities that make a good lover, and then I have them tell me if they have those same qualities. This same procedure can be applied to whatever part of a person's identity they believe needs positive self-esteem. Most people can tell you what their negative attributes are in any area of their self-identity, but to verbalize or write down what they think their positive attributes are makes them very uncomfortable and inhibited.

Why is it so difficult for a person to think, or say, something positive about himself or herself unless it is in the context of a job interview, when it somehow becomes acceptable? The reason for this difficulty is that we are taught at a very early age that we are not supposed to think or say positive things about ourselves. In some way we are told to downplay any positive beliefs; it is important to be humble.

I remember a time when I won a tennis tournament and my name was in the city newspaper. I was all excited and wanted to show everyone I knew. My mother's reaction was to downplay the whole situation. She was a real killjoy. She said, "Be careful, Dan. You don't want to get a big head about this." "Oh, I am sorry mom. I was thinking and saying something positive about myself; I wouldn't want to develop any self-esteem." I didn't say that at the time or probably didn't even realize it at the time, but in hindsight as an adult, it was clear. I generally would become embarrassed that was I celebrating too much—such a sin—and shut down all the joy, and go back into a psychological shell of inhibition. I know my mother was operating as a concerned parent, but it just shows the belief of the time—don't draw attention to yourself, deny yourself, and be humble.

If you didn't follow the rules of self-esteem denial, others would judge you as being conceited, stuck-up, or egotistical. These were labels you wouldn't want in high school; as a result, you couldn't develop your own positive self-esteem. Without a viable means of developing your own internal self-esteem, the only way you could feel good about yourself was through the external validation of others. To attain this validation, you had to perform in some way to get recognition from others. Those who did something well, like being the football star, homecoming queen, the class clown, or the student body president, got some type of positive self-esteem. The only problem with this type of self-esteem is that it is performance-based, and we know that performance can fluctuate, hence so can self-esteem. The bigger problem with performance as the basis of a person's self-esteem is that it's also externally based and doesn't really reflect who they are as person; it's more about what they do: if they no longer can perform that particular activity, they will have no self-esteem.

Some people talk about the concept of positive affirmations, which isn't a bad thing in and of itself. Where I have trouble with the concept is why someone has to keep doing it day after day. Somehow, what they are saying to themselves isn't sticking or becoming a part of their internal belief system. I think that when they say something positive, another voice contradicts what they say and erases the positive statement. As a result, a self-esteem vacuum is created that needs to be filled every day. This can get tiresome.

What I am suggesting is that once you believe that you possess specific positive traits in a particular part of your self-identity, then these traits are established for good. I call this process making your own self-esteem "cake," and what happens externally is the frosting or the lack of frosting; but no matter what happens, you still have the cake—your core self-esteem. Your core self-esteem doesn't change; it's independent of your performance or what others might say to you in the form of compliments or criticism.

Without this core sense of self-esteem, people take external interactions with others on a personal level. It affects them on an emotional level; they take it to heart. Their self-esteem goes up and down depending on performance and what kind of people they interact with in their daily life. This gives others way too much power to determine their self-esteem.

I remember one night my oldest daughter telling me that I was a terrible father because I would not let her stay overnight at one of her friend's house. She went on and on about how I wasn't like all of her friends' fathers. I told her I was sorry that she thought I was a bad father, but she still could not go to her friend's house. If I did not have good core self-esteem about being a father, I might have taken what she said personally, which would have hurt my feelings. I might have caved to her criticism just to gain her temporary approval as a parent and let her do something that may not have been appropriate for her.

Another example of where core self-esteem is critical is in my professional life, whether as a public speaker, a college professor, or a therapist. In all these positions, I expose myself to the criticism of others. If I didn't have a well-established sense of self-esteem in those parts of my self-identity, I wouldn't be able to succeed. Some people will praise me in my professional roles, while others will find fault and attack me professionally. I can't please everyone if I stay true to myself professionally, but my self-esteem as a professional isn't greatly impacted.

COMPLIMENTS

Many people have trouble receiving compliments from others. I was like this at one time. Every time someone gave me some type of positive feedback, I would feel uncomfortable. I would become embarrassed and somehow discount what they were saying.

After I gave a seminar, for example, some of the people who attended would come up afterward and tell me how much they got out of my presentation. I would find myself saying "yeah, but" and pointing out things I could have done better or changed. I was taking away from their experience of the seminar. I just couldn't let the positive feedback wash over me. At some point, I realized that I was negating their perception of the seminar. They had a positive experience, end of story. My different perception doesn't make their experience wrong. Now, when someone gives me a compliment about myself, I give it validity and thank them. This doesn't cost me anything, and after a while if I hear enough positive feedback, I start to develop more self-confidence.

When I give a compliment and the receiver negates or discounts what I am telling them, I get upset with them. This sometimes occurs with my wife when I compliment her about the way she looks. I might say something like this, "Honey, you look so good tonight. I love the way you look." She might reply with, "How can you say that? I am having such a bad hair day!" I usually respond with, "I don't know about that, but to me you look great, so don't take away my compliment."

Some people discount compliments because they don't trust the sincerity or intention of the individual who is giving the compliment. They think that person is just saying something positive because of some ulterior motive. Of course, that might be a possibility, but I recommend just giving face value to the compliment and not questioning the giver's intention. If they have some agenda other than giving you a compliment, you will discover the truth and deal with that fact when appropriate. In the meantime, enjoy the gift.

Compliments are the frosting on our cake of self-esteem. They are an added bonus, but hopefully our self-esteem isn't dependent on positive validation.

Part Two

Making Behavioral Changes that Affect the Way We Love Ourselves

Chapter Seven

Talking to Yourself in a Loving Manner

THE TRANSACTIONAL ANALYSIS MODEL OF SELF–COMMUNICATION

In writing this chapter I need to give credit to Muriel James, Ph.D. She is the author of a book titled *Born to Win*, which was published in 1973. At that time, I was an intern at her counseling center where I worked with teenagers with emotional problems; as a part of my internship, I was offered training in something called Transactional Analysis, or TA, as it was called at the time. This approach became very popular and later faded away from the popular psychology forefront. TA was a very cognitive approach to psychotherapy, which I didn't realize at the time. I took away from that experience some powerful concepts, which I continue to use today. The following is one those psychological models. I have probably made changes to what I originally learned, but at the core, I believe it's the same.

The subject that I want to explore in this chapter is what I call intimate self–communication. In my other book, *Beyond the Marriage Fantasy,* or as it is called today, *Creating the Intimate Connection,* I examined the way couples communicate with each other on an intimate level. So much of couples therapy involves exploring the methods and styles couples use to communicate with each other. I have realized over time that it would be more beneficial to begin therapy by exploring the ways an individual communicates with himself or herself. If people communicate with themselves in a functional manner, then they will do the same with their spouses.

What I like about this model is that it is visual and graphic, which helps people remember and stay conscious in the way that they talk to themselves. When people can remain conscious about the way they speak to themselves, they then have a choice to either continue in the old patterns of self-talk or make changes to improve their sense of self-esteem and emotional well-being.

The TA model is very useful in helping people who have trouble making personal decisions. These are decisions such as whether an individual should get married or divorced, whether she should quit her job or have sexual relations with someone. Often people get confused and lose their way and end up in situations that aren't right for them. They don't trust their own ability to make decisions; and because they lose their confidence, they seek the advice of others, which opens the door to more confusion and inaction. This model can help an individual increase her confidence at decision-making.

In this model, an individual is broken down into three components from which he communicates either with himself or with another person. The first part is called the **Parent**. This is a psychological parent that exists in everyone to some degree or another. This parent part exists whether your actual parents are living or not.

The Parent component is actually made of two types of parents. One is the **critical** parent, and the other is called the **nurturing** parent.

The Critical Parent

The critical parent was established in our psyche as we were growing up in our family of origin. In addition to our family, the culture and geographic area of the country in which we grew up affected our attitudes and beliefs that, in turn, influenced the creation of our psychological parent. Someone who grew up in urban San Francisco would have a different critical parent loaded with different messages than someone who grew up in Charleston, South Carolina. This holds true with people who grew up in different cultures or religions as well.

One analogy for the creation of the critical parent compares our brain to a blank hard drive disk. Our parents, grandparents, teachers, religious leaders, and/or the popular media sat down at the keyboard and programmed our brains with beliefs, rules, laws, and "shoulds" for how to be a person within our family, culture, or society. This is called socialization. Our parents and society did this because they wanted us to conform to these rules and beliefs so that we would be functional people—at least what they thought was functional. So they did this programming with the best intentions. They weren't trying to mess us up psychologically. You might think this by looking back at what your parents' messages were, but they did the best they knew how at that time given their limited knowledge and experience. It doesn't help you now to blame your parents, or anyone else for that matter, for where you are now psychologically. It just puts you in the victim position psychologically, which only leaves you feeling helpless and frustrated about your life today.

When parents and other authority figures in our childhood did this socialization programming, teaching us the rules to be functional individuals, we as children weren't able to differentiate the concepts as to what made sense or what didn't. We weren't able to weed out the functional from the dysfunctional. We just took everything they said as gospel, and we bought everything, completely. In my case, I thought that it must be true if my mom or dad or grandparents said it was true. I didn't question what they said on any level. The questioning and rebelling happened much later in my teens, but by then their messages were embedded in my psyche. Some of the messages were also obsolete. They might have made sense in the 1950s but have little relevance to the present day.

The process of differentiation of the messages an individual received in her childhood and what she believes to be true today is a major developmental step. When an individual can discredit or invalidate a message of her parents and replace it with a new belief, she has truly made the step into adulthood psychologically. It's as if she has passed new legislation that is current for today's times and her own personal life.

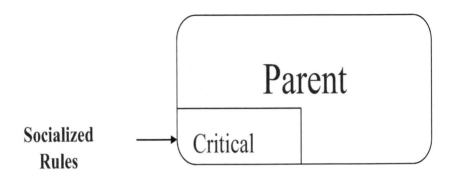

Socialized Rules → Critical — Parent

The Nurturing Parent

The nurturing parent is the other option within the overall parent part of the TA model. Some people have a well-established nurturing parent while others don't, but the potential exists. In defining the nurturing parent, I use adjectives such as loving, supportive, feeding, nursing, accepting, or concerned. Some people can be very nurturing of others, such as mothers and their children, but when it comes to nurturing themselves, they have great difficulty. As a result of this inability, young mothers find themselves drained because they give so much to their children with little coming back to recharge their batteries. The mothers end up emotionally and physically spent, and it becomes more and more difficult to continue to give to their children and especially their husbands. Mothers start developing a great deal of resentment, which they are unable to express because they should be the caregivers and enjoy the experience and keep up the smile. The message is that you don't want to become a bitch, so keep your resentment hidden. It's no wonder that so many women are depressed and take anti-depressants, thinking this is the remedy to the problem. It's only a coping mechanism to deal with being burned-out.

Men often have difficulty understanding the concept of nurturing others or themselves. They think of nurturing as something women do for them or others. When they find themselves alone and divorced without a woman to care for them, they must learn the concept of self-nurturing for survival's sake. Some don't make it and turn to substances and addictive behaviors as a way to take care of themselves.

The nurturing parent skill set can be learned, regardless of gender. It just takes someone who is motivated and open to the change.

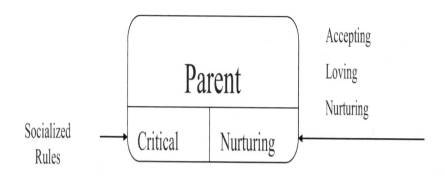

The Psychological Adult, "The Decision Maker"

The adult component of the TA model is the part of our psychological make-up that takes information we receive from the world around us; it processes this information and makes decisions based on this knowledge combined with previous experience, and makes a choice. Hence the nickname the "decision maker," because ideally this is where we go when making decisions— from big choices to mundane ones.

It is not uncommon for a person to have a very functional adult operating in his career or business life, yet in his personal life the adult may not be as developed or involved in the decision-making process. Much of what I try to do is help people develop the psychological adult in their personal lives, regardless of their chronological age. I help them become empowered to set boundaries within relationships and make decisions that are right for them and no one else.

The reason people may have an adult component functioning at work but not at home is because different issues of security are involved—economic or emotional. Many times people have confidence that if they lose their job, there is another one out there for them. They have the confidence that enables them to take the risk of communicating like an adult. This same confidence may not exist in their personal lives, and they feel inhibited to risk adult communication because of their inherent fear of abandonment.

Much of my clinical and academic work involves helping individuals develop the adult component of the psychological repertoire of behavior. This is usually the aspect that is missing and contributing to the lack of intimacy in their marital relationship.

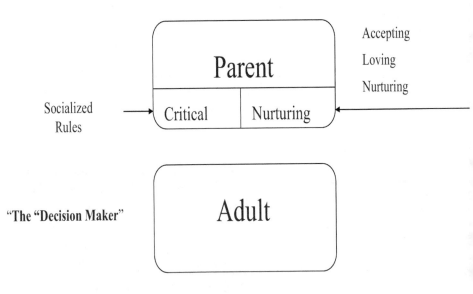

THE CHILD WITHIN US ALL

We all have a psychological child within our psychological make-up, because we were all kids once. The issue now in adulthood is what type of child we were when we lived with our parents. The reason is that this will impact our behavior in an adult intimate relationship. We bring a style of behavior and a set of reactions that have origins in our childhood into our adult personal relationships. We are programmed or conditioned in a way, but this doesn't mean we can't change these behavior patterns once we become aware of them. An individual can choose the old childlike ways or the more appropriate adult choice.

The Adaptive Child

The adaptive child is the most common type I deal with in my clinical practice, but unfortunately, this style of behavior is the source of so many personal and relationship problems. When this type of child was growing up in her family of origin, she was generally the likable kid. She didn't cause too many problems, tried and succeeded in living up to her parents' expectations; she got good grades, went to school, came home when she was supposed to; didn't get into trouble with authority figures; made her parents happy and proud. It's not that there is anything wrong with this type of behavior, except that the child might have a harder time developing her own sense of self-identity, independent of her parents' thinking. This process in psychology is called individuation. It is critical to have accomplished this process before getting into a committed intimate relationship or marriage.

The adaptive style of behavior originating in childhood becomes a major psychological problem when this person commits himself or herself to a long-term relationship, especially a marital relationship. The same adaptive style of behavior that worked for the person as a child carries over into his marital relationship, which lays the groundwork for disaster. I will return to the issues related to the adaptive child behavior.

The Rebel

The rebel is the child everyone is familiar with, because he likes to bring attention to himself by the way he acts at home or in school. This kid does the opposite of what is expected by his parents or society. He doesn't generally rebel across the board, but rather in certain specific areas of his life, usually the ones that are most important to his parents. If good grades and school attendance are important to the parents, then this will be the area in which he will rebel. If the parents want their child to be an athlete, the rebel child will find a way to sabotage his athletic career. The pay-off in this type of behavior for the child is loads of attention, even though the attention is usually negative. As they say, some type of attention is better than none. If a child is reinforced with attention for rebellious behavior, then he will continue to act that way.

The problem is that the child starts to develop an identity of being the rebel and not only gets attention from her parents but also from her peers. We all know how important peer approval and recognition is in adolescence. One way to get peer attention is through rebelling against authority figures. Usually this involves teachers, administrators, or the police. Behaviors of drug or alcohol use, shoplifting, and truancy all fall into this category. As this type of individual moves into her adult years, the rebel child may still exist in the way she leads her life. The individual may not be conscious that the rebel child within her is driving her present-day decisions and adult behavior.

THE NATURAL CHILD

The natural child exists in all of us because we all were two years old once. This is when our entire personality and behavior were completely natural. If you have ever had a child of your own or have been around a two-year-old, then you are fully acquainted with the natural child. The natural child is totally about himself and what he wants now. Natural children don't negotiate; they want it now or else. They can be terrorists right there in the grocery store. The term the terrible twos originates from this type of behavior. You might think that the natural child is all bad and you wouldn't want any part of this type of behavior in your adult life. Most two-year-old behavior is aggressive, selfish, demanding or inconsiderate, but the behavior is not all bad.

I try to bring out two major characteristics of the natural child in all the adults that I work with, either clinically or academically. The first is that a healthy two- or three-year-old reacts to the world around her in a true emotional way. One minute she is happy, and then, in an instant, she can become scared or angry. A two-year-old doesn't have a great emotional vocabulary to communicate her emotional experience, but she feels her feelings—no inhibition, no repressing. Anyone who has had children or has been around a two-year-old has had this experience.

What is the significance of two-year-olds being emotional? As a therapist, it tells me that everyone is an emotional individual or has the potential to be emotional. Another important point related to the natural child and emotion is that two-year-olds react emotionally, regardless of their gender. Little boys react just like little girls. No difference. In the beginning we are all emotional. It's just that boys are socialized to deny that they have emotions and told if they experience them not to share them.

When a male client tells me that he's not an emotional person, I don't believe that. It's what he thinks, but I know if he finds himself in a certain situation or receives certain stimulation, he too will react emotionally. I have witnessed men who haven't expressed much emotion, except maybe anger once in a while, but when their wife of twenty-five years decides to leave them, they have a very emotional reaction. It's as if a Hoover Dam of emotion bursts. They express hurt, sadness, anger, and a great deal of frustration. This same individual claimed not to be very emotional. The emotion had been there all along; he was just really good at repressing the natural child and all his emotions until his wife's leaving pushed him to let go and express what he felt.

The other psychological aspect of the natural child in all of us is that it's highly sexual. Yes, two-year-olds are very sexual, but not in the way you might think. When I say this people gasp, because the idea of a two-year-old being sexual is shocking. I am not saying that a two-year-old is interested in sexual reproduction; they don't have a clue about this type of sexual activity. This is for adults. The type of sexuality that a two-year-old is interested in is physical pleasure. They do things with their bodies that feel good. They touch their genitals whenever they feel like it, they take their clothes off in the supermarket, and they do whatever they want without regard to what is going on around them. The have the natural qualities of spontaneity; they are not inhibited; they don't worry about what the neighbors might think. There isn't any negative judgment in their mind saying don't do this or that. If it feels good, they want to do it. That's what I call natural sexuality.

The potential for this type of sexuality lies within us all. So when an adult client tells me that she isn't a very sexual person, I say. "That's what you think—you just haven't accessed your sexual capacity."

The way many adults tap into their natural child either emotionally or sexually is through the use of chemicals. The use of drugs is a shortcut to the natural child's liberation, at least for a short period. The use of alcohol in particular is the drug of choice to achieve the goal of

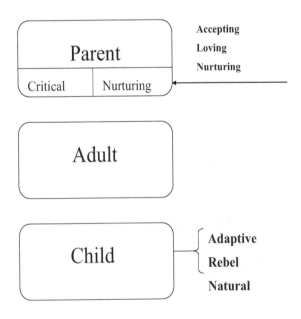

liberation. Alcohol puts the critical parent to sleep so the natural child can come out and party and act silly and uninhibited. All the inhibiting "shoulds" are psychologically blocked until the drug wears off and the self-condemnation begins. When sobriety hits, it's as if the natural child seems to disappear, but it's still there; it's under the oppression of "the critical parent." I don't advocate the use of drugs or alcohol to express your emotions or your sexuality. I would much rather do it through re-writing the psychological programming that keeps these qualities boxed up in an individual's behavioral repertoire.

TOXIC CRITICAL PARENT SELF-TALK

Now that I have described the major psychological components—parent, adult, and child—I want to discuss the day-to-day interaction of these psychological parts. Most people aren't aware of how they intimately talk to themselves. As a therapist, I have become keenly aware of this process. Unfortunately, when people do talk to themselves, often it isn't in a very loving manner, which has a negative impact on their whole sense of self-love and self-esteem.

When I work with couples in therapy, I help them learn to communicate in a way that fosters love and intimacy. If on an individual basis they talk to themselves in a critical, judgmental, or unloving manner, it defeats the purpose.

As a result, self-intimate communication should come first, and then the couple communication counseling, but in reality, it doesn't always work out that way.

In terms of self-communication, the first place I start is looking at the language of the critical parent. The goal here is for an individual to become aware or conscious of this language when using it. When this awareness is achieved, then the individual can make the choice to change the way he talks to himself. Without this awareness, people just operate out of habit without realizing the psychological implications that this has on their well-being.

The language of the critical parent usually is made up of some basic phrases. The first critical parent phrase that I hear frequently is that "I should or shouldn't" do something. I ask this person, "If someone else told you that you 'should or shouldn't' do something without you asking for their input how would you feel?" Most adults would answer that it would make them angry. I don't know too many adults who like being talked to as if they were children.

I am not concerned at this point about someone else talking to you like a parent; my concern is that you are talking to yourself in this way. Generally, when adults talk to themselves with "should," they resent it at some level, or they feel guilt. It's hard to feel respectful about yourself if you talk to yourself as if you're a child. The result is a lowering of your self-esteem.

Another type of critical parent messages are those that start with the phrases, "I have to," or "I've got to," or "I ought to." If you listen to the way people talk to themselves they say things like, "I have to go to the store and shop for dinner," "I've got to clean the house, it's such a mess," or "I ought to spend more time with my kids." On and on we talk to ourselves with these parental messages.

The question I ask my clients and students is what do these messages imply? What makes them parental? The answer is that they imply that there is **no choice** involved, that is, "you have to." It's as if there is a psychological gun at your head with the demand "or else" if you don't follow through. These are all self-imposed demands because we are only talking to ourselves.

With these self-imposed demands, an individual is creating her own psychological prison. This prison is a place where there is little choice and your freedom is taken away. So how is this going to affect a person who lives in her own psychological prison with all these "have tos" and "got tos"? She is going to develop a large degree of resentment and anger. When an adult doesn't feel she has choice in her life, I believe she will build up a great deal of resentment, which can manifest into several negative psychological outcomes. One negative outcome is varying degrees of depression. So many of my depressed clients have over-active critical parents yelling demands at them: "They have to pick up the kids, clean the house, make the dinner, talk to their mother, spend time with their husband and make him happy." I just get exhausted listening to these women. I ask them "Who is in charge of your life? No wonder you are depressed and exhausted all the time. Living under that psychological oppression would bring anyone down." I hear this same type of talk from the men I work with, although their "have tos" and "got tos" might sound different.

I believe that the self-imposed label of being a procrastinator comes from this type of critical self-talk. A person who believes that he is a procrastinator keeps telling himself that he either has to or must do a particular task, but he doesn't seem to get around to doing it. At an unconscious level, he resents the demand/no choice aspect of the self-talk. In a passive-aggressive way, he resists the critical parent in his head and rebels like a teenager and doesn't accomplish the particular task. He

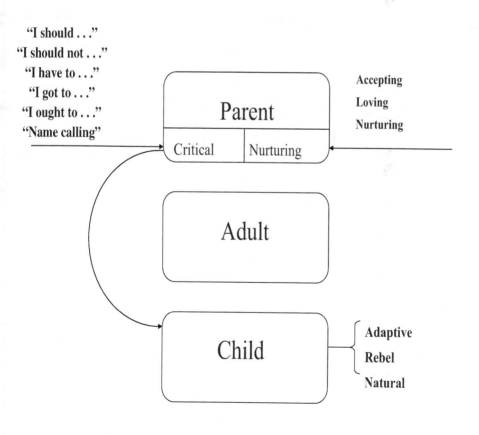

rationalizes all of this with the label of being a procrastinator. "What can I do about it? I guess that's just the way I was born." I don't think so, sorry.

The last verbal weapon in the critical parent's arsenal is the use of self-imposed critical names. It's amazing the names that we call ourselves. We say such things as "I am so stupid," "I am so fat and ugly," "I am so irresponsible," "I am such a lazy person," "I am an idiot and a failure." On and on it goes.

The emotional impact of this type of self-talk is that we are psychologically hurting ourselves. It destroys our self-esteem and self-confidence. It's truly not the way you would communicate with someone you love.

Breaking the Pattern of the Critical Parent

With most of the adults I work with in therapy or the students I teach in college, I tell them that at this point in their lives they have received plenty of parenting. Their critical parent has been programmed to the max since they have been children, but now they are adults, at least chronologically.

It's time to communicate like an adult. They need to communicate from the standpoint of the psychological adult, not the critical parent or their child. The adult phrase I suggest they use is traditionally called an "I message." More specifically, I suggest they use the verbal phrase *I want or I don't want*. This is what an adult says when she is expressing her desires.

As an adult, I only do what I want, because I am in charge of my own life. I call the shots. I am responsible for the actions and choices I make, no one else. I am one hundred percent accountable. This is what being an adult is all about on a psychological level: accountability.

Now I can imagine some of you reading this thinking that I can't just do what I want. There are certain things that you have to do if you want to be part of this society. I don't *have to* do anything. It's always a choice, but with every choice, there is a payoff and a consequence. If I want to rob a bank I can, but I choose not to because of the consequences, which may include being removed from society by spending my life locked up in jail. No thanks. Some adults might make a different choice and go for the pay-off, but the cost is that they are now spending their lives in prison.

Some of you might think this adult approach to life sounds very self-centered. It's all about you and what you want. What about others and their desires and feelings? Don't you care about other people? The answer to these questions is a profound yes! I care about others because I don't want to be self-centered or insensitive. If I wanted to be that way, my consequence of living in that aggressive manner would be that I wouldn't have many friends or a healthy intimate relationship. I would probably be lonely, and my self-esteem would be in the dumpster. Unless you are a sociopath, this is a very high psychological price to pay for choosing not to care about others.

For some people, just knowing what they want in this world is hard to figure out. They are so concerned about pleasing others that they never take the time to ask themselves what their desires are. It's just easier to forget about their desires over time. Knowing what you want sounds easy, but it can be difficult for those who have been playing the adaptive child role for a long time. The idea of saying what they want can be overwhelming and threatening at the same time. Stating what they want makes them vulnerable, and they don't want to be that exposed, especially in an intimate relationship.

For others, knowing what they want is challenging because they never developed their own desires. They don't ask themselves what they want. They don't have a backlog of experiences in which they have defined themselves in terms of desires or interests. They have a whole lot of potential for discovery, which can be exciting, and a whole new possibility for adventure in their lives. They have the opportunity to truly define their own sense of identity.

The challenge for an individual who wants to communicate with others from the adult psychological position is having confidence, knowing that his desire is right for him. The developing adult doesn't know how to make the right decision in terms of what he should do or if what he wants is right for him. He has little confidence in his choice-making ability, due to his lack of experience in making choices for himself. None of this is related to chronological age. This process of moving psychologically from the child to an adult can occur anytime in a person's life.

The developing adult's natural tendency is to ask others what she should do. Often in therapy clients will ask me what they should do. They ask questions such as "Should I get married?", "Should I quit my job?", "Should I get divorced?", or "Should I sleep with my boyfriend?"

People want me to tell them what to do with their lives. They want me to tell them what the best choice is because I am the professional therapist, just like the direction a parent would provide for a child. If I told them what I think they should do, I would merely enable them to be dependent and prevent them from developing the confidence to be adult.

I respond to the client's questions by saying that if he were in a room with six other people, they all would have different opinions as to what you should do with your life. All their opinions are related to their background and experience and may not have much relevance to your life. If the client listens to others, he will become confused, not knowing what direction to take. I could tell the client what I would do, but that doesn't mean it's right for him.

The response I give to clients when they want me to tell them what they should do, for example, whether or not they should get married, is to ask them the question: "How do you feel emotionally about getting married today?" What I look for is whether they feel *comfortable* or *uncomfortable*. If they respond with, "I am uncomfortable getting married today," then I tell them their answer is that they are not ready to get married. The client might react and tell me that her parents think that she should get married, that the time is right, and her fiancé is such a nice guy. I tell her that I don't care what her parents or anyone else thinks about it. If someone isn't comfortable, then they need to listen to their feelings. It's time to operate like an adult. How many people have walked down the aisle with the feeling in their gut that they are not comfortable with what they are about to do, but they don't listen? After they are married, they are critical of themselves and say, "Why didn't I listen to myself? What a mistake I have made, because now I want to get divorced." This process applies to whatever the subject might be, and a decision needs to be made to resolve the conflict. In order to move forward, an individual needs to feel emotionally comfortable with her choice.

If the client tells me that he is comfortable with getting married, then I say, "Great, go forward. You most likely will not regret your decision, because it's the right one for you." It's such a simple process, and yet so many people find it difficult to make personal decisions. We are not taught as children to listen to our feelings; we are taught to listen to the directives of authorities.

Once the child leaves her family of origin, she is on her own and is now held accountable for her choices and actions. But many of us are not taught how to be psychologically in the world as an adult. It's kind of a sink or swim process. Unfortunately, we live in a very complex adult society, and with more options and choices confronting us every day, so many young adults today feel overwhelmed. Many retreat and live with their parents when they need to be out on their own. Some make the wrong decisions and find themselves in some type of trouble because they weren't prepared psychologically for the adult world.

When I ask clients how they feel about a particular choice and they respond with "I am confused" or "I am not sure how I feel," then I tell them that they aren't ready to make a choice. They don't have the clarity of emotional direction. It's like a client saying, "One day I feel very comfortable about getting divorced. Then the next day I am not comfortable with the idea." I know divorce attorneys run into these clients all the time. When they see confusion in their clients, hopefully they refer them to therapy to resolve their confusion before going through all the expensive legal process, only to have the client change his mind.

When an individual is emotionally confused or conflicted, she doesn't have the clarity of direction to make the right choice in terms of some desire or action. How long does it take to achieve enough emotional clarity or consistency to be able to make the right choice? The time it takes to wake up and feel the same way consistently depends on the person and the situation. In other words, there is no "right time."

Whatever time it takes to achieve emotional clarity is the right time for that person. If you or someone else puts pressure on yourself to hurry up the process, to force a decision before you are emotionally ready, your decision will usually backfire. Did you ever say to yourself that you wished you had listened to your gut feelings after you committed yourself to some action?

I see this situation occur when a couple is separated and the husband can't stand being in limbo regarding his marriage. His wife isn't sure about whether she wants to reconcile, and her husband wants back in the worst way. He pressures her by saying, "You have had enough time to make up your mind," but this pressure only makes his wife more confused and resentful. Everyone has his or her own timeframe in making decisions. There is no right time, just whatever time works for you.

When I encounter a client who is confused about what is the best path to take and he is impatient with his indecision, I tell him that he needs to do more emotional research. Usually people who are on the fence about a decision make a pro and con list, either in their heads or on a piece of paper. This is an intellectual exercise that doesn't help speed up the process in making major life choices. It helps, but this approach has its limitations.

What I mean by emotional research is that people need to have more of an emotional experience regarding their decisions. Having the client "ramp up" his emotions usually speeds up the decision-making process.

Take the case of John who has been married to his wife Karen for twenty-five years. He has been separated for about six months and is trying to avoid filing for divorce, but he just can't seem to do it. It would be so much easier if he could go back to his wife, children, and their lifestyle, but he can't make himself comfortable at home, since he had an extramarital affair with a woman he met at work. The affair is over, but he is still confused about his marriage.

I advise him to do some emotional research by taking his wife to Hawaii for an extended weekend. After his trip, he should have more "emotional data" that will help with his confusion. Being with his wife for an extended period time will give him the clarity he is seeking. If he is bored and finds himself looking at the other women at the pool, wishing he were with them, then that ought to tell him something. On the other hand, if he and Karen are reconnecting intimately, talking about how they feel about each other, and making love, that will show him another path. Either way, the experience is going to speed up the decision-making process.

Making adult decisions requires that a person be aware of what she feels emotionally. If an individual is not in touch with her emotions, she may have a hard time making correct personal decisions regarding her life's path. This is why people who use substances such as alcohol or marijuana find that they later regret decisions they've made, because they lacked the sobriety to make good choices.

When someone is in an area of his life where he has never been before, his emotions are his personal compass to point him in the best direction. Knowing that a person has this compass takes a lot of anxiety away from venturing out into the world, whether this new area is physical or psychological.

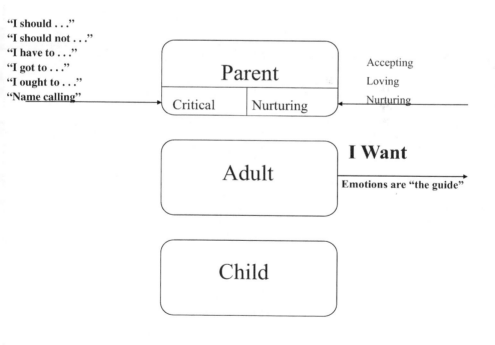

A real-life example in which I help my clients apply this concept of listening to their emotions is when I have a divorced client who finds herself single after twenty-five years of marriage. She is out in the dating world and is scared and lacks confidence. The idea of dating again is daunting; she doesn't know the rules or the expectations. When she asks me for advice, I tell her the rules and expectations aren't important. What is important is how she feels about what's happening to her. Just because another adult wants something in the single world doesn't mean he is going to get it if she is not comfortable with his desire.

REWRITING "THE SHOULDS" OF YOUR LIFE

So often I hear people in my office say to themselves that they "should do something"; and when they don't, they tell me that they feel guilty. Guilt is a common emotional experience of adults that usually has a negative impact on their emotional state. An adult usually experiences guilt either when he thinks about or actually does something that is in conflict with his belief system—his own personal set of rules that are part of the critical parent in his head.

When a client tells me she feels guilty about something in her life, I ask her what rule or "should" she is in conflict with. For example, one of the classic guilt messages or "shoulds" that many people, including myself, had embedded in our critical parent was that "**You shouldn't hurt other people's feelings.**" This is especially true for women. Women often tell me that they don't want to hurt a man's feelings. They censor their truth. I ask, "Why don't you tell him that you don't want to go out with him?", or "Why don't you tell him that you don't want to have sex tonight?" Typically, she answers, "I don't want to hurt his feelings." My response is, "How did you become responsible for the emotional well-being of another adult?"

In this case, the "should" that an individual should not hurt someone emotionally is the rule that is carried within the critical parent. I had this "should" operating in my psychological makeup. I am not sure how it was programmed into my brain, but the "should" existed nonetheless. The effect it had on me was that I couldn't express myself; it inhibited me from expressing myself because I might say something that would hurt someone emotionally.

The concept that one shouldn't hurt someone else emotionally is dysfunctional. To liberate myself from its tyranny, I made a new rule or belief that stated that I am going to hurt someone emotionally. I can't control the outcome of what I say or what I do. In other words, how someone reacts or interprets what I say or do is his choice. It's not that I want to intentionally hurt someone, but when I speak the truth and take that risk, I can't ever really control the other person's emotional reaction.

Changing the belief or "should" from how we were raised to creating a new "should" or belief that we want to live with is a major psychological growth step in becoming an adult. This change represents cutting the psychological cord with your parents. I am not saying that everything needs to change, but the rules/"shoulds" that are obsolete or dysfunctional need to change so that the guilt is removed, and you are no longer in conflict with your past programming.

Some other dysfunctional "shoulds" I have changed with my own critical parent are the following: **I shouldn't make mistakes; this would draw attention, and I would be embarrassed**. The result was that I couldn't learn or participate in activities where I would make mistakes. I didn't allow for any type of learning curve. The result of this "should" was that I didn't grow in any new areas; my growth was stunted. The replacement belief was: "Of course you are going to make mistakes; it's normal when you try something new and everyone else who has attempted the same task has had the same experience of making mistakes. We all were beginners once."

Another old "should" that ruled my life when I was younger was: **I should get everyone to like me, especially women**. This is a very difficult task to accomplish because in reality you cannot get everyone to like you as a person. Believing that everyone should like you creates an unrealistic expectation that only leads to a great deal of social performance anxiety. I was always a nervous wreck in social situations in which

I had no previous experience with the people involved. This "should" inhibited me from participating in social opportunities, and when I was involved with people, I came across as very shy. When I was dating women, I did whatever I could to get them to like me. I could never just be myself, because there was too much risk that she wouldn't like the real me. To liberate myself from the social oppression that this caused, I had to rewrite the rule/"should" to state that you can't get everyone to like you, but if a few people like you, that's all you need. They really like you for who you are, not some phony version of yourself. You don't have to pretend, so you can relax and have a good time.

Another "should" I remember from my childhood programming that my mother said was: **"If you start something, you shouldn't stop until you finish the project."** This might have worked if I was always single and didn't have a family and other conflicting projects and involvements. An example of when this "should" didn't work was when I would start a Saturday morning landscaping project and work all day until I couldn't see anymore because of darkness. I would be proud of what I accomplished, but my family was upset because I didn't spend any time with them that day. I couldn't fully enjoy the fruits of my labor because of the guilt of ignoring my family. The "should" from my mother was an extreme position with no middle ground. I needed balance, so I gave myself a break, saying, **"I could start a project and stop even though it wasn't finished and focus my time on something else."** That way, I wasn't resentful Monday morning going in to the office because I had worked on some project all weekend and felt like I didn't have any fun. The project would still be there next Saturday, and I could work on it some more. It didn't have to be finished in one day. The project might take longer to complete, but I would have a more balanced life with a change in the old dysfunctional belief.

I hope you get the idea of how to set yourself free from the tyranny of the critical parent "shoulds." I don't believe that you can totally erase these old messages completely, but you can create an antidote belief to offset the past that will enable you to live in the now without the guilt.

The Psychological Prison of Our Own Making

Other types of critical parent messages that have a negative impact on a person are the phrases, "I have to" or "I've got to" or "I ought to." People use these words in their everyday communication, and they don't realize the implication of what they are saying to themselves. Phrases such as, "I have to clean the house," "I have to do the shopping," or "I have to make the dinner," sound innocuous to most people, but there is an emotional cost when they are used.

Implicit in saying "I have to," "I've got to," or "I ought to," is that there is no choice. These sound like demands with no alternative. This sense of demand or lack of choice creates the emotional reaction of anger or resentment. I don't know too many adults who like to be spoken to as if they are little kids; it's going to make them angry. The same reaction occurs when an adult talks to herself in the same manner; she will develop some level of resentment.

Is the individual who is using these self-directed critical parent statements aware that he is causing himself a certain level of resentment? I don't think he is conscious of what he is doing. Usually he notices the symptoms, with the number one being different levels of depression. Another symptom is a lack of motivation to get the things done that he tells himself he has to do.

These self-directed critical parent messages give the user a sense of powerlessness, because on a subtle level they take away choice over what is happening in his life. He feels he isn't in charge, and that someone else is calling the shots. The individual isn't usually aware that this process is going on, but it can affect his outlook on his life.

Children don't have choice when it comes to living with their parents and doing household chores. When I told my daughters to unload the dishwasher, I didn't expect them to ask whether my request was fair, convenient, or optional. I was making a demand as a parent. This is appropriate within the parent-child context, but to speak to a lover in this way is inappropriate and will create little intimacy between the couple.

CALLING YOURSELF CRITICAL NAMES

How often do you call yourself critical names or hear others judge themselves? It goes on all the time, but why do we do it? When you call yourself "stupid, ugly, idiot, fat, skinny, irresponsible, lazy," and a whole lot worse, what's the purpose of this type of self-communication? What would be the emotional impact if a lover called you those names? It would hurt like hell. Well, when we call ourselves critical names, we hurt ourselves as well.

When we experience this pain, it usually turns to anger, which can be directed to others, especially those close to us, in inappropriate ways. A person can internalize or hold in the anger, but this saps her overall energy level, which will have a negative impact on her motivation to take on the tasks of daily life. We generally label this condition depression.

When we call ourselves names, I don't believe that we are trying to inflict pain on ourselves. We think pain will motivate us to create some kind of change in our lives. The truth is that it backfires and undermines change. I will explore this further later.

All the critical parent messages I have discussed—"I should," "I have to," "I've got to," as well as critical name- calling—yield only negative psychological outcomes. I don't see any use for them. Most adults have been parented enough, and now it's time to communicate intimately like an adult. This in turn will have a positive outcome in how we communicate intimately within the context of an adult relationship.

When Seeking Harmony Turns to a Nightmare

In this section, I want to revisit the issues related to the adaptive child in many adults' psychological makeup. When an individual was a child in his family of origin, acting in an adaptive way probably served him psychologically. It gave him a strong sense of security and peace of mind that is essential for healthy childhood development. This adaptive approach to childhood works when a person is a child, but when he brings this same adaptive approach to a committed adult lover relationship, it spells psychological disaster.

Having harmony in an adult relationship is usually seen as a good quality. Couples often brag to me, "We don't have any conflicts. We never fight." When I hear this kind of statement, I know there is trouble in paradise. There must be conflict within their relationship unless the couple are clones of each other, and that situation is one that I haven't yet experienced. This sense of harmony means that they avoid communicating what's true for them regarding their desires or anything that might upset the harmony of the relationship.

The consequence for this adaptive behavior for the individual is that she is unable to be her true self within the context of a committed intimate relationship. She is unable to feel a sense of freedom to express herself. People walk around on eggshells—always afraid that they might say or do the wrong thing that might upset their partners.

Over time in a long-term relationship, the adaptive partner will lose his sense of self. He won't know his own desires, tastes, or interests. He will become something that he thinks his partner wants in a spouse. He has lost all sense of individuality within the context of his intimate relationship—like a psychological prison. This is not to say that an adaptive person doesn't have a sense of self outside of the context of his relationship. He might be a very different person around his friends or when he is involved in a work setting, but when he comes home, it all changes.

The psychological and physical costs of this personal adaptive behavior are tremendous. The inability to really be herself in her personal life causes a great amount of resentment, anger, and hurt. The issue is that this adaptive approach to living within a relationship doesn't allow for the healthy expression of these emotions. People generally have to internalize, repress, and deny what they really feel. Eventually this emotional approach is going to create all types of psychological problems.

The most common of these problems is depression. Living in a psychological prison is depressing. An adaptive person has to internalize his anger, which just wears him out physically, because it takes a great deal of energy to hold back anger. The adaptive person acts lethargic and complacent, and just loses his passion for life in general. Adaptive people lose their sexual desire and interest in their relationships, even though they always show up. They are there physically, but just not emotionally. They are merely going through the motions of their lives, which may seem functional on the surface, but the happiness and passion for living is missing.

The impact on a marriage is also devastating, but only the trained eye can spot the damage. On the surface, the adaptive individual looks normal, and everything is always fine. If the surface is scratched, however, it's a whole different story. It is hard to trust this partner. You never know what is real about her. You don't know if she is doing what you asked because she wants to or just to keep the peace. Without this type of trust, it's impossible to develop any type of real intimacy.

It's impossible to be intimate with an adaptive individual in a relationship, because he doesn't allow you to know him. He believes it's too risky to put his true self on the line. What you get instead is a manufactured person, the "Stepford" wife or husband. He seems like everything anyone would want in a partner; he is so "nice and caring," which makes this act all very seductive. But what is the psychological price tag? After a period of time, the act seems real, but in truth, it's still an act.

The conflict between the true self and the adaptive self within the individual creates a great deal of anxiety. Acting in one's personal life creates a constant state of stress, because one is always on stage. The adaptive individual is always afraid that at some level someone is going to discover that she is not being truthful in her personal life. The anxiety levels start out slowly, but gradually increase. As the amount of anxiety increases, so do the symptoms.

Adaptive individuals develop different coping mechanisms to deal with their anxiety levels. They like to stay incredibly busy in many different activities, most commonly their children, if they have any. They just can't sit still, because if they do, they will feel anxiety or anger for not allowing themselves the freedom to be themselves. They may stay busy cleaning, or engaging in the classic "retail therapy." These mechanisms are all normalized within our culture, so no one is going to make any judgments regarding these activities.

One coping mechanism that can create judgments is the use of alcohol. Initially, consuming alcohol is not necessarily a problem, but as the anxiety levels increase in the individual's life, the use of alcohol may also increase. Problems start to occur related to drinking. The person gets his first DUI or ends up drunk at a neighborhood party, embarrassing himself or his spouse and not remembering what happened the next day, or driving his kids' carpool under the influence. These are common signs that an alcohol problem exists.

Besides the use of alcohol as a way to self-medicate anxiety, the adaptive individual may turn to a doctor for prescription medications. These drugs are very helpful at alleviating the symptoms of anxiety, but do not address the underlying problem that produces the anxiety in the first place. The anxiety continues, and the need for the medications increases, which can lead to addiction to prescription medications, a major problem in our country. If medication is used, it must be used in conjunction with psychotherapy.

Given all the negative consequences, why would a person take this adaptive approach to living in an intimate relationship? Clients usually tell me that it's just easier, they don't want any fighting or arguing to occur, and they want peace and harmony in their relationship. If I scratch

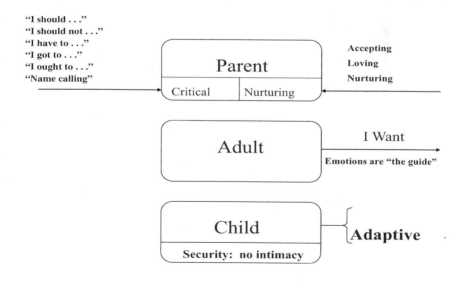

the surface of these answers and ask what the big deal is if they have conflicts or that an argument occurs in their relationship, they can't really connect the dots at first. Then they start talking about their fears, which include the loss of love, the loss of approval by their partner, and then the ultimate fear: that their relationship will dissolve and they will end up alone. The so-called psychological payoff for adaptive behavior is that it offsets the fear of abandonment, at least in the moment. It gives an adult the sense of *security*.

This security is really an illusion, because as I stated earlier, only you can give yourself real security. Any adult can abandon you at any given time; that risk always exists, and to think otherwise is to live in a sense of denial that will be difficult to handle when reality hits. Your partner could have an affair, fall out of love with you, and leave you for someone else, no matter how adaptive you have been in the relationship. They could also get some disease and die and leave you alone in this world. Adaptive child behavior does not work in sustaining the life of a marriage.

Break Out of the Psychological Prison and Become Adult

If you find yourself in the adaptive child pattern of behavior in your intimate relationship, how do you break out and seek the freedom you desire? You want to, because you love yourself too much to keep yourself locked up in a prison of your own making. The psychological path out is to move from the adaptive child to becoming the psychological adult. Easy to say, but it takes courage to make this change happen in reality.

To break free and make the shift from the adaptive child to the adult requires the desire to take the risk not to control the outcome of how your partner may react to your *truth*. Take the risk that if you communicate what is true for you, your partner might get mad or angry. They may not like who you are and ultimately leave you, but if they don't, then you have the chance to have a real intimate relationship that isn't manipulated by adapting to keep the peace. Do you want intimacy or a false sense of security? The choice is yours.

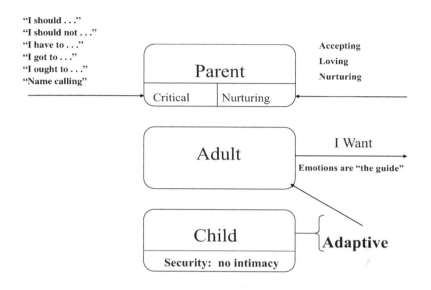

Taking the risk to be vulnerable and communicate the truth creates the potential for real emotional intimacy, which sets up the possibility of being in love with your partner, as opposed to just loving them. It allows for true passion to be present, which in turn spills over into the couple's sexual relationship.

Being Self-Critical Will Only Bring You Down!

The last area of self-communication I want to discuss is the way that individuals talk to themselves in a self-critical manner. You hear it all the time if you listen. People put themselves down about their performance in some activity because it doesn't meet their standards or expectations. They call themselves names that are demeaning and critical. They may literally yell at themselves, thinking this will be helpful in some way.

In my past, I was very critical of myself in whatever endeavor I approached. I yelled at myself when I played tennis, swore at myself, called myself critical names. I said things like: "What a stupid shot. You are such an idiot for playing that way. You stink." If I lost the match, I would be down on myself the rest of the day. It's as if I was playing at the U.S. Open and for lots of money. Whether I won or lost really only mattered to me, and in hindsight, it was a small event in the big picture of life. It's important to be passionate about what you do, but there needs to be a balance and perspective.

My self-critical approach would not only occur on the tennis court, but would also happen in my therapy office. One common example of this would be when I double-booked appointments for clients. I would walk out of my office, go in the waiting room for the next client, and see two people waiting to see me at their scheduled time. They could read the expression on my face and know immediately what I had done. I had to make a quick decision as to who I was going to see and who was going to be rescheduled. The clients were generally understanding, but I was terribly embarrassed. For the next couple of hours I would internally berate myself for my mistake. It would sound something like, "How could you be so disorganized and unprofessional?" "I can't believe you could make such a mistake and inconvenience your clients. It's just being irresponsible." No one else knew that I was talking to myself this way, but my mood showed that something was bothering me. It might take me a couple of hours to stop the scolding, and then I could be present again.

Why did I talk to myself in such a self-critical way when I was upset with my behavior? What was the intention behind the self-critical talk? What was I trying to accomplish?

Most people aren't really conscious of their intention. The self-critical talk has just become automatic behavior for them, a habit. On further examination, they usually decide that their intention is to motivate themselves to improve or change their behavior to correct whatever they are doing so that it won't be repeated.

When I yell at myself on the tennis court for not performing to my expectations, I somehow think that I am going to play better. The truth is that I don't perform better; in fact, I play worse. The more that I am critical of myself, the more performance anxiety I create for myself. Performance anxiety cripples optimum performance. In sports vernacular, an individual "chokes" or freezes, which in turn only creates more anxiety and lowers performance. It becomes a vicious downward spiral.

In the other example of yelling at myself for double-booking my appointments with clients, I thought that if I was self-critical enough, maybe I would stop making this mistake. After all the years of private practice, I still occasionally make the mistake of double-booking. So all of the yelling at myself in the past was ineffective at changing my behavior.

Being self-critical does not promote personal change; in fact, it creates resistance to changing one's behavior. When I was in training as a therapist, we were taught not to be judgmental of our clients. If an atmosphere of judgment exists within a therapeutic relationship, it wouldn't be safe for the client to become vulnerable. Judgment inhibits an individual to take risks, which is essential for personal growth and change to occur.

What if I talked to a client in this judgmental fashion: "Wow, you are really a screwed up, sick individual." Instead, I could say, "Well it looks like you have some problems. Which one would you like to tackle first?" Quite a contrast between the two approaches. The first one would probably turn the client off therapy and they would never come back. The second approach encourages the client to work on his issues without feeling condemned or judged for having problems.

The opposite of being judgmental or critical of yourself is to be accepting. When you accept your behavior, it doesn't mean that you're happy about what you did, but you don't put yourself down to where it ruins your self-esteem and destroys your self-confidence. I learned this conceptual difference between being self-critical and self-accepting as it applied to the therapeutic relationship, but for some reason, I didn't make the transition to my personal life right away. It's not an uncommon experience with therapists, but I found it hard to live with that contradiction.

Where I noticed that I was using the concept of acceptance in my personal life was after my two daughters were born. As their father, I got to watch many of their activities, including competitive tennis matches. I was one of those parents rooting for their kids from the sidelines. After a match, if they lost, they would be very self-critical of how they played.

Instead of chiming in and telling them how badly they played, I told them to give themselves a break. I would say things like, "Well at least you gave it your best shot. After all, you're only fourteen, and there wasn't any money riding on the outcome." Basically, I was telling them to accept the result, and not to beat up on themselves for their performance.

Then one day, I had the "Ah-ha" moment, the big epiphany that I didn't talk to myself in the same way.

I was hard on myself when was unhappy with my performance. I never gave myself a break; there was no self-acceptance; just be critical and judgmental—that's what I deserve, I thought.

Then I realized that I wasn't very loving to myself by being so self-critical, calling myself names, and putting myself down all the time. I was accepting and loving of my daughters but just the opposite with myself. Once I realized what I was doing, I started to hear that critical voice inside and stopped it dead in its tracks, replacing it with a more nurturing parent voice that said, "Give yourself a break. You're not perfect, and you are going to mess up and make mistakes. After all, you're only human." I finally started to treat myself with self-love in behavioral terms through my self-communication. And I finally started to accept myself as I was at that moment in time.

This didn't mean that I was happy when I screwed up and made mistakes; it just meant that I didn't destroy my self-esteem in the process. The irony of this shift in attitude was that when I was more self-accepting, I made fewer mistakes and was able to have a more relaxed approach to life in general.

Another by-product of self-acceptance is that when I am less critical of myself, I am less critical and judgmental of others, which enables me to be around people who have different beliefs and attitudes, including political views or musical tastes. When I was self-critical, I would put people down who were different from me in any way. As a result, I was only comfortable around people who were essentially clones of me. Everything had to be the same. How boring—there was no diversity, and no growth. Today I can be around people who are different from me, which in turn enriches my life with a more varied and enriched life experience.

Chapter Eight

The Anger Model: How to Use Anger to Create Positive Change

COGNITIVE DISSONANCE THEORY AS A WAY TO LIVE IN PEACE WITH A CRAZY WORLD

So often I hear the term anger management used when it relates to an individual who seems to express the emotion of anger in a destructive manner. One expert in the field of anger management, Leonard Ingram, says that, "One out of five Americans has an anger management problem. Anger is a natural human emotion and is nature's way of empowering us to 'ward off' our perception of an attack or threat to our well-being. The problem is not anger; the problem is the mismanagement of anger. Mismanaged anger and rage is the major cause of conflict in our personal and professional relationships."

This chapter discusses my professional approach to dealing with the emotion of anger. The attitudes and behaviors that individuals use when handling their anger can play a direct role in influencing their self-esteem and their sense of being a victim in the world, which in turn impacts whether they are psychologically loving themselves or not.

The first belief that I want address is that anger is somehow a negative emotion. On the contrary, anger is a useful emotion in that it acts as a catalyst for personal change and growth. As I discussed in my first book, *Creating the Intimate Connection,* all emotion is good if you are going to pass judgment. It's not the emotion itself that people usually judge, but the way that the anger is communicated, or how it gets expressed behaviorally. We live in a culture that teaches that anger is bad, and therefore we don't learn how to deal with anger in any effective positive manner.

We are taught not to have the emotion of anger, which puts us in a major double bind. Anger is a natural response, but at the same time, we are told not to express the emotion. How many times did I hear my parents say, "Dan, if you don't have anything nice to say, then don't say anything at all." This statement always frustrated me and created even more anger.

We do not learn effective methods of managing anger as children; as a result, when we reach adulthood, we only model negative methods for the next generation, and the pattern continues. Because we have been taught that anger is negative or bad, when we experience anger, we try to find ways not to feel it. We want to deny, repress, ignore, and avoid having this so-called negative emotion. When I ask clients where the anger goes, they say that it just goes away over time. They think that the anger they are experiencing just somehow dissipates into the atmosphere.

Many people think that working out in the gym is a good way to deal with their anger, as if the anger goes out their pores with their sweat. The reality is that none of these methods of repression work to resolve anger. It will just sit in a "psychological underground," building up until an explosion occurs. If there is no explosion, then this method of internalization will create a condition of depression for the individual.

Directing Anger in a Way That Produces Positive Change

In my therapy practice, when a client comes in for their first session, they usually present a situation they are involved in where they are experiencing a great deal of hurt and anger. The situation could be their marriage, their job, or their relationship with an in-law. Within that therapy hour, the client identifies what specific behaviors or experiences cause their anger. I call these the "client givens". The givens are not open for debate; they are the client's perceptions or experiences. Many times other people want to negate or discount the client givens, but for that individual, it is always true, even if others don't agree.

Often when a woman comes in to see me and talks about her marriage, she mentions common complaints or givens that she says make her angry: "My husband doesn't communicate with me about his emotional experience," or "He doesn't listen to me when I am upset." "I think my husband is cheating. I don't trust him, and he denies any infidelity when I confront him." "We never have any sexual activity unless I make it happen." "He always gets stoned or drunk when he gets home from work." When she is in a relationship where one of these givens is occurring, the woman is going to be angry and or hurt.

The next issue is what clients do with their anger. I ask them where they direct their anger. What is the focus of their anger? Usually they direct their anger at their spouse or partner. They may do this in two ways: either by verbally expressing their emotion to their partner, or by expressing their anger inwardly to themselves about how they feel about their partner.

Generally, communicating your anger to your partner in a constructive manner is the most positive approach in keeping a relationship intimate. Where this communication of anger becomes a problem is when you repeatedly tell your partner about what they are doing that upsets you and makes you angry, but they don't change their behavior. They hear you, but they continue acting in a way that upsets you or hurts you emotionally.

If, after you have communicated your anger verbally in a constructive manner, your partner doesn't change their behavior, I would advise you to stop directing your anger at your partner. You are wasting your anger, and just throwing it away. Why? Because if you direct your anger at someone or something you don't have any control over, it will leave you in a helpless position to bring about change. You will feel powerless, frustrated, and even angrier than before.

A good example of this is when a spouse tells her husband that his drinking is upsetting her and causing her a great deal of resentment. The wife has mentioned this repeatedly, but he keeps on drinking, because he doesn't think he has a problem. He thinks that his only problem is that his wife keeps nagging him to stop drinking. If she would just shut up about his drinking, his life would be great, he thinks. Unfortunately, you cannot get someone sober; only they can change their drinking behavior.

Another path a spouse might take in dealing with her anger in a relationship is to direct it at herself. The anger comes out as self-criticism for being involved in such a dysfunctional relationship. She tells herself that she is stupid or dumb for staying in a relationship where she keeps getting hurt and angry. She thinks that getting angry will somehow motivate her partner to make the necessary changes to better their situation.

The psychological reality is just the reverse. When individuals direct their anger at themselves, they usually end up being depressed; and when they become depressed, they lack the energy to make changes in their lives. They are tired, down, and blue, and they become apathetic about everything, except maybe going to sleep. Getting angry with yourself only immobilizes you from making changes to better your situation.

Directing anger or hurt at a person or partner more than a few times only leaves a person powerless at resolving their anger, and directing the anger at themselves leaves them feeling helpless to change their situation. . The individual ends up feeling like a victim—powerless and helpless as an adult. It would be difficult to have good self-esteem or self-love if a person found himself or herself in this position. Many of my clients come into therapy in this exact situation, seeking my help to improve their relationship.

The Path to Empowerment and Change

The path out of this sense of powerlessness or being the victim of the situation is to direct their anger at something they have control over. If someone is in a relationship with a person who lies, or verbally abuses them, or drinks every night to oblivion, then they need to be angry that they live in such a relationship. Don't get mad at yourself for being in the relationship, and don't get mad at your partner for all the things they do, but get mad at the relationship. The relationship is dysfunctional and unacceptable, and you can remove yourself from the situation. As an adult, you have the choice, or control, as to where you live; it's up to you. Your power exists to change things for the better.

It sounds so simple if you are unhappy and angry at the situation—you can just leave and find happiness. If that were really the case, I would lose half my clients. What keeps individuals in unhappy situations such as an unhealthy or toxic relationship? The answer is the emotion of *fear*. Fear is what keeps people from changing their life situation. Fear inhibits or blocks an individual from making changes in their life. Some of the common fears that I deal with in my practice that keep people in unhealthy marriages include the following: I am not sure how I will be able live on my own either emotionally or financially. If I leave, I am afraid of how it might affect my children. I am fearful that others will see me as a failure if I get divorced. I am fearful of living alone the rest of my life.

These are common powerful fears that can psychologically trap an individual in an unhealthy relationship. This has nothing to do with love. The individual is not in the relationship because they are feeling loved, supported, respected, or fulfilled; they are staying because of fear. When someone is in a relationship out of fear, it's really not a choice. It's like a "shotgun wedding." This psychological intimidation is mainly self-imposed.

Can a person truly commit to a relationship when their choice is driven by fear? The answer is no. There is a relationship, but from an emotional point of view, that individual has "checked out." She may go through the motions, but living this way makes it impossible to form any real experience of emotional intimacy.

The inability to experience intimacy in your relationship and the sense of being trapped in a marriage by your own fears will feel like your own personal prison. Emotionally, you will experience anger, hurt, and frustration, and you will most likely end up feeling extremely depressed. So many clients come into therapy feeling this way.

It's as if this individual is in the middle of the scale of justice, with anger and hurt on one side of the scale and fear of leaving the relationship on the other. These emotions drive the person's decision-making, not the logic and all the pros and cons of staying in the relationship. It may be helpful to analyze the situation, but ultimately it's an emotional decision. I have frequently seen clients who tend to be very analytical in their approach to decision making in their daily lives, which may work for them in their business or professional lives, but when they use this same approach in their personal lives, they can become paralyzed.

When a person's experience of anger or hurt reaches a level where it outweighs their fear, then at that point they are motivated to make the necessary changes to resolve their anger and hurt. How much anger and hurt a person has to experience before he or she makes the change needed to better their situation depends on the individual. The amount of fear that has kept the individual stuck in his or her situation will also determine the amount of anger required.

An example of this dynamic is a wife who has been unhappy in her marriage but too afraid to leave, because she isn't sure if she can live alone as a single adult. Then one day she comes home early from work and finds her husband in bed with her best friend. She is so angry and hurt with the situation that she moves out of the house right away and doesn't let her fears get in her way. I hate it when people to have to experience more anger and hurt, but sometimes that's what it takes before they are willing to make personal changes to better their lives.

I prefer to help clients reduce their fear level so they don't need to go through any further anger or hurt to make personal changes. I have them confront their fears and talk about them about how they might mitigate the impact of their fears. Generally, this requires getting information to see if their fear is based in reality. Ignorance is the parent of fear. An example of this process of enlightenment is where a woman's husband has threatened that if they get divorced, she won't get a dime of support from him, or that if she leaves she will lose custody of her children. These statements are meant to prevent her from leaving him. He knows what her fears are and is playing on them. All these fears can be relieved by one visit to a divorce lawyer to see what her real rights are under the law.

Just talking aloud about these fears with a therapist can reduce their inhibiting power. The fears may not go away completely, but this process may give a person enough strength to take the action needed to move through their fears and change their situation for the better.

When the anger and hurt increase to the point where they outweigh the fear, usually at that point a person has the emotional motivation to make the changes necessary to remove herself from the toxic situation. If the fear on the other side of the scale outweighs the degree of anger and hurt, then generally the fear will block the person from making the changes, and they will stay stuck in an unhealthy situation.

Cognitive Dissonance Theory, the Key to Freeing Yourself of Consistent Anger

Sometimes a person finds himself or herself in a situation where they don't want to leave, but at the same time, they don't want to be angry. This may be an employment position where there are things about the job that makes a person angry, but because they want the money, they don't want to quit and walk out. At the same time, they don't want to be angry every time they go to work.

Another situation where we might not want to participate is when we have to get together with certain relatives or in-laws every so often at holidays and special events. These relatives may act in ways that can get us upset and angry in a very predictable manner. We might prefer never to see these people, but because they are related to us or to our spouse, we interact with them.

The antidote for these situations and many others is the understanding of two psychological concepts. The first is that we make ourselves angry. Other people and events just provide the stimulus to which we choose our emotional reaction. There are situations where we instinctively react with anger. These events seem to come out of nowhere, and we just emotionally react. In these situations, we don't have much time to think about our emotional reaction. These situations happen repeatedly, and are fairly predictable.

This can be a hard concept for people to understand, because they want to blame others and situations for their anger. They think that it's the other person's fault: the teacher, the parents, the girlfriend, the boss, and so on. On the contrary, an individual can choose to respond with anger if they are responsible adults. The good news is that if we are responsible for making ourselves angry, then we also have the power to choose not to react with anger.

I am sure there are situations and events that you generally would react to with anger, but after a while, you may say to yourself, "Why bother? It's just not worth getting upset." Changing a cognitive belief also changes our emotional reaction. This example illustrates the second concept known as **cognitive dissonance theory,** a psychological method of resolving anger. I originally learned this theory as an undergraduate in sociology at the University of California, and have continued to apply it my entire career.

Cognitive dissonance theory translates to "mental noise." It's like the difference between playing a C major chord on the piano, which sounds harmonious, and pressing random keys simultaneously, which sounds like a lot of noise. The noise in the brain, so to speak, creates our anger.

In fact, an individual has cognitive beliefs and expectations as to how they want their reality to exist. When their actual experience and their expectations or cognitive beliefs don't match up and collide, the individual experiences dissonance, which causes them to become upset and angry.

A common example is people who go around with the cognitive belief that the world should be fair. In a perfect world, this concept would be true, but unfortunately, the world isn't perfect, and it truly isn't fair. So when someone with this belief sees or experiences injustice, they get angry and upset. These people tend to be angry a lot, and aren't always fun to be around. When I encounter them in therapy, I confront their belief about the world and fairness. They live in a constant state of dissonance, which can take a toll on them both physically as well as mentally. They are stressed out all the time.

I have many clients who experience a great deal of cognitive dissonance. A typical case is a divorced mother, Jane, whose child spends the weekend with her father, Jane's ex-husband. Jane comes into my office complaining that her ex-husband Frank feeds her daughter too much sugar by giving her cookies and ice cream whenever she wants. This makes Jane extremely angry. She expects Frank not to give their daughter sweets because she has told him not to on many occasions. She expects that when she communicates her resentments about something Frank is doing that he will change. Jane's expectation or belief sets her up to be angry. She has two cognitive beliefs that are in conflict with her reality, because Frank keeps giving their daughter sweets and doesn't change his behavior when Jane tells him that it upsets her. The conflict between Jane's expectations and reality causes her to react with anger.

In therapy, I tell Jane that she can get angry all she wants, but how effective is it to get mad at Frank? She and I can both agree that feeding their daughter sweets isn't a good idea, but I point out to Jane that she lacks the power to change Frank's behavior or the situation. Her constant hope that he will change keeps her in a state of disappointment and frustration. She could go to family court, but the judge isn't going to deal with this type of parenting issue unless it's life threatening to the child.

This brings Jane to the critical point involving the concept of cognitive dissonance and her anger regarding her situation. She has choices that can make a difference in her emotional experience. Her *first* choice is to keep expecting or hoping that Frank is going to listen to her and see how angry she is about his behavior and stop giving their daughter sweets anytime she wants them. Her *second* choice is to remove herself completely and walk away from the situation. Jane could do this by not having contact or knowledge of what Frank is doing with her daughter when she spends weekends with him in accordance with their custody agreement. This choice doesn't seem very realistic, given that Jane doesn't want to abandon her relationship with her daughter and is very concerned about what happens when her daughter spends time with her father. Jane's *third* choice is to resign herself to the fact that Frank isn't going to listen to her concerns or her anger and is going to keep doing what he wants regarding the parenting of their child, and that's the reality of her situation.

The third choice is the one I suggest to most clients who find themselves in a situation that they don't see leaving the situation to relieve their dissonance/anger, and when they don't have the power to change the circumstances or the individual with whom they are involved. What I suggest they do is change their expectation to be in line with the reality that they keep experiencing. By changing their expectation, they won't be in conflict with their situation, and therefore will have harmony and will not be angry. Accepting the given reality doesn't mean that you approve or that you are happy about the situation; you just won't be angry.

A personal example of the last choice stems from my experience as a father. When my two girls were in their last years of high school, they were pretty messy, and would leave their belongings all over the house. This seems to be standard adolescent behavior these days. I thought that when they got older, girls especially would be neater, but I was wrong.

I would spend several hours before I went to work cleaning and straightening up the house so I had it just the way I liked it. I expected that when I came home from work, it would be the way I left it. Unfortunately, my two daughters had been home from school for several hours, and the place was a mess by my standards. Their books, backpacks, clothing, and any dishes were left where they used them. I would flip out, become very angry, and yell at them to pick up all their stuff. They would give me their usual attitude, responding with "I will do it later, Dad," or "Why do you have to be such a neat freak," which would only get me more enraged. This approach wasn't working at resolving my problem. I couldn't intimidate them as my parents had done with the threat of physical punishment, because those days are gone. I didn't want to kick them out of the house at that point because I knew in a few months they would be going off to college to live in their own places. I wanted to appreciate these days, because I knew it was the end of an era in our parent-child relationship. At the same time, I didn't want to be blowing up with anger every time I can home from work. What was a father to do?

I applied the very principle that I tell my clients and students about— cognitive dissonance theory. It was time to practice what I preached. I changed my expectation that the house was going to be the way I left it when I went to work to expecting the house to be a mess with stuff left all the over the place. When I came home and encountered the mess with my new expectation, I didn't react with anger. I just said to myself, "What else is new? Did you expect a clean house?" This doesn't mean that I was happy or didn't have a problem that needed to be addressed. I just didn't blow up and yell, but in a firm direct manner, I instructed my girls to take care of things, and I didn't get as much attitude back from them. I was not giving my power away by allowing them to make me angry. Changing my expectation wasn't easy at first, because it really wasn't what

I wanted, so I needed a way to remind myself so I wouldn't forget when I walked in the house. To keep me from forgetting, I put a sticky note on the dashboard of my car that said, "Expect mess," and sure enough, that's what I encountered when I got home. But instead of exploding, I said to myself, "What do you expect?"

In summary, an individual has three choices when they experience cognitive dissonance:

- First, they can live in the conflict and stay angry. They are unwilling to change their expectations, but they stay in the conflicting situation.
- Their second choice is to remove themselves from the conflicting situation and therefore hold on to their expectations, but not be in conflict or anger.
- Their third choice is to change their expectations to be in harmony with the situation, thus resolving the stress and their anger.

Constructive Direction of Anger

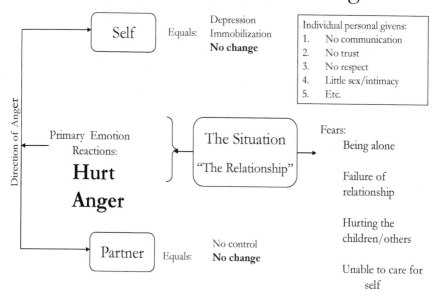

Chapter Nine

Cognitive Distortions: Beliefs That Set You Up for Low Self-esteem and Other Mental Problems

This chapter deals with an individual's beliefs about themselves or others that cause them psychological difficulty. These beliefs are called cognitive distortions. When we have some type of negative experience, the critical parent inside starts beating us up with negative statements, like "You will never be any good," or "No one will ever like you." After saying these critical statements to ourselves repeatedly, we start to believe they are truths, and our beliefs become distortions.

These critical beliefs become absolutes with very little research or any objective perspective. They become directly responsible for generating dysfunctional emotions and their resultant behaviors, like stress, depression, anxiety, and social withdrawal. Our feelings follow what we are thinking, and negative thoughts like these can send us spiraling down into depression.

When a cognitive distortion becomes an individual's belief, they hold it to be a truth. They then use this belief as a way to view their world. It becomes what's called a cognitive filter. This filter dictates the choices they make and the actions that they take in their everyday lives. They filter the experiences they have or what they see happening in their world to reinforce their distorted belief.

For example, a woman might believe that all men have extramarital affairs. She uses this belief as a reason not to get married. Every time she hears about someone cheating in their marriage, either in her own personal interactions or in the media, she uses that information to reinforce her distorted belief. She might say, "I told you all men cheat—they just can't be trusted." Of course, she filters out all the relationships where men who don't cheat, and only focuses on those men who act out in this way.

The way to overcome cognitive distortions is through a process called cognitive restructuring. The first step in this process is to recognize the detrimental beliefs and the impact that they have on a person's life. The second step is to learn how to challenge the distorted beliefs and their relationship to reality. The last step involves replacing the distorted beliefs with more self-enhancing beliefs. Cognitive restructuring is very similar to the re-parenting process discussed in Chapter Seven regarding the Transactional Analysis Model of interpersonal communication.

The first step in overcoming a cognitive distortion is to become aware of what you might be saying to yourself that is causing you difficulties. Here is a list of the typical cognitive distortions.

OVERGENERALIZATION

An overgeneralization is when a person states a belief to the extreme. There is no middle ground or gray area. An individual takes an isolated case or experience and then uses that example to make broad generalizations.

Phrases that start with words like never, always, all, none, or no one are common examples of overgeneralizations. Statements such as, "No one likes me," "You never say that you love me," and "I always have to take out the trash," are examples of this type of cognitive distortion. If you confront the accuracy of someone's overgeneralization with facts and data, they will get upset and defensive. The discussion almost becomes like a court of law where both sides argue the credibility of their beliefs. The problem with this approach is that they are not parties in a court of law; they are in their own living room, and no judge or jury are going to make a ruling on who is right or wrong. The debate usually goes nowhere.

Whether or not the overgeneralization is true, the person making the statement believes that it's true, and at that moment in time, they are having an emotional reaction to their belief. How they feel is real for them, regardless of the accuracy of their belief. To communicate effectively with someone who makes an overgeneralization, the first step is to give validity to their emotional experience, regardless of whether you question the accuracy of their belief.

One prime example for me occurred when my younger daughter, Michelle, was an undergraduate at the University of Colorado. One night we were talking on the phone, and she told me that all the boys at the university were jerks or something to that effect. As her father, I was tempted to say, "That can't be true. What are you talking about, Michelle? Have you talked to all those thousands of boys on that campus and have found them all to be jerks?" This is what I wanted to say, but I was aware enough not to go down that road. If I had told her that her overgeneralization was wrong or inaccurate, she most likely would have become upset and defensive and refused to talk to me anymore, and hung up the phone. This experience often occurs between parents and children as well as married couples. The communication breaks down and problems develop.

The more effective path I took with my daughter was first to give validity to how she felt, even though I thought that her belief was a cognitive distortion. I said, "I guess it's going to be a pretty lonely semester if all the boys there are jerks. You must be feeling sad and frustrated, because you thought it was going to be different socially." Her response was, "Yeah, Dad, that's right, you understand." That's where I left it with her—no problem solving or fixing. I was there for her in a supportive way and allowed her to be in a funk. The next day, she called me and said that she had met this really nice guy in her math class, and she was in an entirely different mood. I didn't confront her about her cognitive distortion from the day before; I was happy that her reality had changed, both from an attitude and emotional point of view.

Global Labeling

Global labeling is a cognitive distortion where an individual forms a stereotypical attitude or belief about entire groups of people. The most common type of global labeling I hear are phrases that start with, "all women" or "all men." For example, "All women just want a guy who has money," "All women are too emotional," "All men cheat in committed relationships," or "All men just care about how a woman looks physically." When someone makes these statements, I would like to ask them, "How many men or women did you interview to formulate this belief?" I wouldn't actually do this, because I know that they would likely get defensive and hold on to their position. Attacking a cognitive distortion usually doesn't work until the emotional charge connected to the belief is acknowledged.

Global labeling can also be used to perpetuate racist beliefs. Of course, these stereotypes have no validity in reality. When an individual repeats these phrases enough, they start to believe them to be true. When children hear their parents make statements about whole groups of people, they believe what their parents say without question; if their parents say it then it must be true. This is how racism and prejudice continue to be passed down from one generation to the next. I hope this is changing.

Self-Global Labeling

Instead of labeling a whole group of people, individuals sometimes label themselves with a cognitive distortion that can have a negative impact on their self-esteem. They say that they are lazy or stupid, and after saying this a number of times, they start to believe that what they are calling themselves is actually true. It becomes a self-fulfilling prophecy. As with most cognitive distortions, if you tell the person what they are calling themselves isn't accurate, they will probably become defensive and disagree with you.

As a therapist, I take these beliefs apart so that the client can see the inaccuracy and the damage their belief is having on their self-esteem. When a client says they are *stupid*, I respond with, "You say you're stupid, but you have a master's degree in accounting. Tell me, how does that work?" They may respond, "Well, I am stupid because I stayed in a marriage for so long when I knew it wasn't healthy for me." Generally, people who tell themselves that they are stupid do so because they aren't happy with their behavior or the decisions they have made in their personal life. The therapeutic connection I make for them is that most of their decisions were made because of certain fears that they had at the time. In many situations, fear trumps intelligence. After the fact, it's easy to look back and judge our decisions, but at that time, we could have been overwhelmed by fear. Our fear motivated the decision-making, as opposed to our intelligence.

Another common put-down is when someone calls themselves *lazy*. "I am just a lazy person." When they talk this way, it's as if somehow they were born with the lazy person gene. There is just nothing they can do about their "lazy condition;" it's beyond their control to change. My usual response to this label is that I don't believe I have ever seen a "lazy person" in my clinical practice or in my personal life. I have seen people call themselves lazy, but they work forty hours a week. They may have situational laziness, but they definitely aren't lazy people.

So if there aren't lazy people then what do you call people who just sit around the house lounging on the couch, eating, and watching TV all day? People who call themselves lazy are most likely not motivated. They don't have the "fire under their ass" to get off the couch and make something happen for themselves. They just use the lazy label as a cop-out, so they don't have to take responsibility for their choice to sit there all day on the couch.

When I work with a client who says they are lazy, and I help them break free of the self-labeling, they can then see that their action or lack of action is about choice and decision-making. They can then take ownership of their choice and not blame some fictitious condition called laziness. They will become aware of the forces involved in dictating the choices they make. For example, they may realize that it's their fear of failure that keeps them from filling out the application form and getting a new job. It's not that they are lazy; they are just not motivated because of their fear.

Another example of self-labeling is individuals who view themselves as being *stubborn*. Again, they use this label as if they have some kind of condition called being stubborn and there is nothing they can do about changing it. It's as if they were born stubborn, or that being this way is a part of their genetic makeup, or their being stubborn has something to do with the astrological sign that they were born under. They believe that they are helpless to change their behavior that creates the cognitive distortion.

The dictionary defines stubbornness as being unreasonably obstinate, or fixed or set in purpose or opinion. This sounds like someone who just wants it all his or her way, and doesn't want to negotiate or compromise about anything. To me, this type of behavior and attitude sounds like a choice of how a person wants to be in the world. This approach might work if the individual lives alone, but I don't think it will work in relationships with others. This individual rationalizes this choice with a label, as if there isn't anything they can do about their actions. The last common self-labeling cognitive distortion is being a *procrastinator*. If someone views themselves as a procrastinator, it usually means that they put off activities or responsibilities to the last minute. They delay taking action until the deadline is looking them in the face. A classic example is when a person waits to do their federal income tax return until April 14th—the day before the return is due to be filed with the government. If you confront this person and ask them why they waited to the last minute to do their taxes, they will tell you it's because they are a procrastinator. They are implying that being a procrastinator is a part of their identity, and there isn't much they can do about it. They can't be held accountable for the way they act.

Procrastination is a choice, not a condition. Procrastination is similar to the label of being lazy; they both have to do with the issue of motivation. Someone who tends to procrastinate becomes motivated to do a task only when they have no other option but to get the task done. Also, the consequence of not accomplishing the task by a particular date motivates them to complete it.

When I was a senior in college, all my finals were take-home final exam papers. I had a job waiting for me as soon as I was done, so I was in a big hurry to finish my papers so I could get to work and make some money. I got those papers turned in on the first day of finals. It was an understatement to say that I was highly motivated. On the other hand, I had friends who were in no big hurry to get back to their hometowns and summer work. They put off doing their papers until the last day of finals week. Did they procrastinate or make a choice based on different levels of motivation? I believe it was a choice related to their motivation.

Filtering

Filtering is a type of cognitive distortion where the individual tends to focus their attention on the negative of anything and to filter out any positive aspects. It's almost as if the individual with a filtering distortion becomes blinded to anything positive when they are focusing on the negative aspect of an experience or object.

The filtering distortion does major damage to a person's self-esteem as well as to their body image. They constantly acknowledge their limitations, liabilities, or flaws. As a result, it's hard for them to believe that they have any positive self-esteem. Again, just like the other cognitive distortions, if you confront the distortion, the person will just argue to defend their belief.

An example of filtering would be spending all day cleaning your house and getting it spotless. When your spouse walks in, you say, "Look at how clean the house is. I worked on it all day." Your spouse replies, "I see that you cleaned the house, but you missed a spot over here on the floor." If you didn't understand the cognitive distortion, you may take this type of feedback personally and get extremely angry and frustrated, because all your positive efforts and results weren't acknowledged—only the flaws. No one is perfect, so there are always going to be flaws. Sometimes the person with the filtering cognitive distortion is labeled as someone who sees the world as being half empty as opposed to half full.

Filtering also has a negative impact on body image. Through our culture's exposure to the media, we see images of men and women's bodies that generally look perfect, with no flaws. These images are doctored to look this way because perfection is an ideal that we strive to obtain. We are brainwashed to believe that if we buy the right products, then this look of perfection can be ours for a price. The problem is we can't be perfect, because we are human, not machines. The individual with the filtering distortion will always focus on the physical flaw and negate the rest of their physical attributes. As a result of this internal censoring of perception, the negative self-belief reigns over the person and creates constant body-image insecurity.

When you tell them that they look attractive, they will come back with, "No I don't; I have this stretch mark right here" or "I am too big here or too small there." They can never feel good about their body, because all they see are the imperfections, and they can't appreciate their assets.

Polarized Thinking

The cognitive distortion called polarized thinking occurs when an individual views reality in extremes. It's all or nothing, black or white—no gray. Either you are the best at something or you're the worst. A person with this cognitive distortion is unable to make balanced judgments of themselves or others.

The sad consequence of polarized thinking is that it is very damaging to an individual's self-esteem and to anyone that they may be involved with. They are what I call very toxic people. Stay clear of them if you can, because they will only bring you down psychologically and you will get little support. They can be especially damaging as parents in terms of their children's self-esteem.

When polarized thinking is involved, the individual will always judge themselves as inadequate, never good enough, or even worse, a failure in whatever endeavor they pursue. This is because with polarized thinking they have to be perfect at whatever they do to receive positive self-validation. Again, people aren't perfect, so polarized thinking will always end up making them feel inadequate. The same perfectionist judgment they apply to themselves often ends up being directed at everyone else around them.

When people I meet find out that I play tennis, they often want to know how good I am. If I looked at that question from a polarized thinking point of view, I would have to say that I am a bad tennis player. Why? Because I am not number one in the world. I hope that this sounds like ridiculous thinking. I am a good tennis player at my level and age range, but there will always be better players, and there are also those who don't have my skill level. There are degrees of competency in every aspect of life—it's the gray zone.

When applied to oneself or to some significant other, the polarized thinking cognitive distortion can be incredibly intimidating when taking on some new challenge. This thinking creates an enormous amount of performance anxiety for the individual who is taking the risk of doing something new. That person believes they have to be perfect right out of the gate. They have no learning curve to develop their ability over time, or to make mistakes and learn from them and develop any confidence regarding the new task or activity.

If a person believes that they have to be perfect or they are a failure, then they probably won't take the psychological risk of doing anything new in their life. The consequence of not wanting to take this risk is that a person stops growing and ends up stuck. They are unable to move out of their comfort zone, and they become stagnant.

In my practice, some single clients ask me, "How can I meet other single people other than on the Internet?" I suggest to them to try to get involved in some sports activity like recreational softball or volleyball. They might meet someone they could have a relationship with, or they may just have a good time hanging out with people out to have fun playing a sport. The polarized thinking client will respond that they are not good enough to play, because they haven't played since high school, and they are afraid of the judgment of others. So instead of being able to expand their social network, they are blocked by their cognitive distortion.

When this polarized thinking is applied to marriages, it can have another crippling effect. Some people are afraid to get married because of the high divorce rate. A polarized thinking person looks at the institution of marriage as a success or a failure. Knowing how many people fail at marriage, it's so intimidating that they can't make the commitment to get married. They have no way of guaranteeing the outcome of the marriage, so they avoid the commitment so as not to fail.

There are also people who have made the commitment to marriage but see leaving an unhealthy relationship as failure, so they stay and feel trapped and depressed because of their cognitive distortion. As their therapist, I try to show them that they can't fail at something they don't have complete control over, because a marriage involves another person, and they probably also received little if any training on how to have a successful marriage.

Self-Blame

This is a distorted thinking style that has you blaming yourself for everything—whether it's your fault or not. People with this distortion tend to say that they are sorry all the time. They are sorry for anything that goes wrong: if it rains on your parade, they are sorry; if your girlfriend dumped you, they are sorry; if you didn't like the movie they told you about, they are sorry. You can tell them that it's not their fault, and they will still tell you that they are sorry.

They tell you that they are sorry because they take responsibility for everything, as if they have some control over the outcome of all events and experiences. This is different from having normal empathy for a person's emotional experience. A person with the self-blame distortion takes on inappropriate responsibility. If their marriage dissolves, from their point of view, it's their fault, and they are totally to blame. This might be true if they were married to themselves, but the marriage involved another person, and they had no control over their partner's commitment to the marital relationship.

Someone with the self-blame cognitive distortion ends up feeling a great deal of guilt because they take inappropriate responsibility for people and situations. You might ask yourself why anyone would want to take on all this responsibility. Why would they want this burden? The answer is because if they believe they are completely responsible, then they think they have control over people and situations. It's this need for complete control that drives them into this type of distorted thinking. Of course, they end up feeling totally out of control because of all the negative things that occur that they can't control.

Personalization

Personalization is a cognitive distortion that occurs when an individual believes the world is focused on them. In their view, they are the universe and all others and events relate to them in some manner. They see themselves as the cause of some negative external event or experience. In reality, of course, they probably have nothing to do with the outcome, but their distorted belief says they did.

What is the psychological consequence of personalization? The individual ends up with little sense of power over their environment. They see themselves as a victim of all the negative events that around them. Because of this sense of helplessness, they can end up feeling various degrees of depression. Their self-esteem is negatively impacted because they treat everything that isn't working out for them or others as if it's their fault, and their self-esteem is directly connected to their performance.

Someone who has the distortion of personalization lives under a tremendous amount of pressure, because when they are out in public, they believe that everyone is watching what they are doing. This pressure translates into a great deal of anxiety, which in extremes can contribute to different forms of social phobia.

I once had a case with a client named John. I was trying to help overcome his fear of flying so he could travel long distances. He needed to be able to get on an airplane, because he wanted to go to Club Med in Mexico for a singles vacation, and he lived in San Francisco. Generally, when someone has a fear of flying their main concern is that the plane will crash and they will die. They don't want to give up control to the pilot and be vulnerable. In John's case, it was for a very different reason.

John had the cognitive distortion of personalization, and we talked in-depth about the causes of this problem and how his beliefs were distorted; but this approach wasn't working in terms of reducing his fear of flying. After many sessions of psychotherapy, I realized that the only way to confront his distortion was not through intellectual discussion and insight, but through experience. He used his intellect and his distorted beliefs as a defense against having to be out in the world. He would talk a great line about how much he wanted to go to Club Med and meet single women, but deep down he was scared of leaving his home base where he felt somewhat secure. The reality of leaving his comfort zone raised his anxiety levels so much that he became inhibited from making any changes in his life. He wouldn't come out and say that he was afraid at that level, but that's what was really occurring.

My approach was to create a realistic situation to confront the cognitive distortion head-on. I was going to fly with him to Los Angeles, have lunch, and then fly with him back to Oakland. Besides leaving his comfort zone of his home base, he also had a fear of being in an airplane for an extended period of time. He wasn't afraid that the plane was going to crash; his fear was that everyone on the plane was going to be watching him and paying attention to his every move. He was worried if he had to throw up, cough, burp, or pass gas that everyone on the plane would know, because they were all watching him. In his mind, he would be on stage, and there was no way out at thirty thousand feet. This sense of being trapped creates another level of anxiety and is an example of the cognitive distortion of personalization operating in a highly crippling way.

I could tell John session after session in my office that the passengers on the plane weren't going to be paying any attention to him, but his belief wouldn't change. He needed to hang on to his belief for defensive reasons that he wasn't able to admit.

We had a plan, and he was to make the reservations to fly to Los Angeles. The date was set and we were ready to leave. But at the last minute, just before we were to leave for the airport, he came down with a cold. It took three attempts at getting to the airport before we finally got on the plane. It can be hard to confront your fears and move through them.

Once we finally made it onto the plane, John and I buckled our seat belts and waited for takeoff. He was so anxious, and kept asking me if the other passengers were looking at him, and I reassured him that no one was paying attention. Of course, this exchange occurred several times until the plane was in the air. Once we were in the air for a while and at our cruising altitude, John asked me once more if any of the passengers were looking at him. I assured him again that they weren't. As I had told John many times before, these people had their own affairs to worry about and didn't care what he was doing unless he did something that was a direct threat to their safety.

He seemed perplexed that his belief wasn't playing out in the reality of flying, and I was there to witness the experience, which gave it more validity. Then came the big surprise: feeling frustrated that people weren't paying attention to him as he feared they would, he stood up and told the flight attendant that this was his first time flying, and everyone started applauding and giving him all this adulation, and he just beamed a big smile.

After this initial flight and further therapy sessions, John's personalization distortion had less power over his inability to fly. He was able to fly to Club Med in Mexico and met a woman there, and developed the confidence to travel on airplanes.

The cognitive restructuring attitude I use to replace the crippling effects of personalization is to tell the client not to give their power away to what others may think. Do not allow the beliefs or judgments of others to prevent you from living your life to its fullest. In John's situation, he was giving his power away to all the passengers on the plane to inhibit him from having a good time at a resort, because he thought that they were all observing and judging his every action, even though they weren't.

Mind Reading

The cognitive distortion of mind reading happens when an individual believes that they know what everyone else is thinking. They can go to a party and think that they know what everyone there is thinking about them. They assume that everyone else shares the same opinions and judgments. If the individual thinks that they look great tonight, they assume that everyone else must think so too. In some way, this gives the person with the distortion a certain amount of comfort because they aren't challenged by diversity of thought or opinion. When everyone thinks like you, life could become a little boring with everyone being clones of each other in terms of their thinking.

Mind reading becomes a problem when a person projects their own negative self-judgments onto other people. They assume that since they think they look bad, everyone else shares their view, because everyone thinks the same way. The mind reading assumption can be rather overwhelming unless the person has good self-acceptance, because every time they judge themselves negatively, they think everyone else judges them the same way. This distortion would create too many critics in the room for any sense of comfort.

The person who makes these assumptions never checks out the reality of their beliefs. They interact with others without finding out what they truly think. Even if they realized that their assumptions were incorrect, they probably wouldn't believe that they are being told the truth, because they want to stay with the cognitive distortion that they can read minds because it gives them a sense of psychological safety out in the world.

Control Fallacies

With this cognitive distortion, an individual may have a false sense of omnipotent control, or the opposite, that they have no control at all—everyone else is in control. As the therapist John M. Grohol states, "If we feel externally controlled, we see ourselves as helpless, a victim of fate." For example, 'I can't help it if the quality of the work is poor, my boss demanded I work overtime on it.' The fallacy of internal control has us assuming responsibility for the pain and happiness of everyone around us. We might ask someone, "Why aren't you happy? Is it because of something I did?"

When an individual has an omnipotent sense of control, it gives them the feeling that they aren't vulnerable in a world that has many variables that are out of our control on an everyday basis. If they constantly focused on this fact, they would experience a great deal of anxiety. One way to offset this reality of vulnerability is to create a distorted view where a person thinks they are in total control of everything, when of course they're not.

When experiences happen to someone with control fallacies that cause them to become aware of their lack of control, and their sense of vulnerability is revealed to them, they tend to react with anger and fear. They are in conflict between their belief that they should be in control and their experience that they don't have control over everything. They blame others and the world and make the shift from feeling in total control to becoming a victim of the world. They feel helpless, powerless, and depressed. There is no balance of control—they either have it all or they have none. Polarized thinking distortion combines with the control fallacies distortion.

One cognitive restructuring belief I use to help people with control fallacies is a version of the Serenity Prayer that works for the individual regardless of their beliefs related to God and higher powers. I don't use the whole prayer, just the part that follows:

God/Higher Power, grant me the serenity
to accept the things I cannot change;
Courage to change the things I can;
and wisdom to know the difference.

This mantra is a great way to keep our sense of control in the world in a healthy balance.

Chapter Ten

The Behavior Patterns of Being Passive, Aggressive, and Assertive and How They Shape Our Self-Love and Intimacy with a Lover.

B ack in the early 1970s I first started hearing the term "assertive" with regard to an individual's behavior. I didn't learn the concept as an undergraduate in psychology or even as a graduate student in counseling psychology. I started learning it from women who I knew at the time who were involved in the Women's Liberation Movement. These women saw themselves as feminists and realized that being assertive was a way for them to free themselves from the other two traditional choices of acting: being aggressive or passive. Historically women only had the choice to be passive, but feminist women wanted nothing to do with being passive as many of their mothers had been. They also didn't want to adopt the role of being aggressive, because they had watched their mothers live under the oppression of their aggressive fathers. This is not to say that all men were aggressive, but this was the expected behavioral style for men, and in many ways, this hasn't changed.

Being assertive became a political statement, and was part of a social movement with the intent to change women's roles within our culture. Soon books were published outlining what it meant to be assertive. *Your Perfect Right* and *I Feel Guilty when I Say No* are examples of books that led the way at that time. It seemed that assertiveness training groups were being held everywhere, at least in the San Francisco Bay area. Most of the attendees of these courses were women, but some men took the classes as well.

As we moved into the 1980s and beyond, the whole assertive behavior concept seemed to go away, at least as it related to couples and individuals.

I am not sure why this happened. Maybe everyone became assertive and there wasn't a need for more books and classes. From my experience, at least clinically, I haven't seen a drastic change among the women I work with when it comes to being assertive, although there has been some change when compared to the pioneers of the early 1970s. Most men still need the books and classes, however, because unfortunately, they seem to be stuck with only two options: passivity or aggressiveness, with the latter being the preferred choice.

The goal of this chapter is to describe the three behavior patterns of being passive, aggressive, and assertive, and the role each plays in affecting a person individually as well as their impact on an intimate relationship.

PASSIVE BEHAVIOR

The first behavior style I want to discuss is passive. Other names given to the passive style of behavior include easygoing, laid-back, going with the flow, mellow, and my favorite—being nice. Generally, these labels have a positive connotation. The truth is that there are severe negative consequences to passive behavior within the context of a personal life.

The Characteristics of a Passive Individual

The main feature of a passive individual is that they deny their true self. They deny any emotions that may be judged as being negative. They don't allow themselves to be angry, upset, hurt, or frustrated, at least not externally. They take these emotions and suppress them. Their goal is to always put on a positive front, no matter the consequences for themselves.

Another form of the passive individual's denial is in terms of what they want. The last thing they will do is to tell you what they really want. They will always try to defer their true desire. If they are asked what they want, they respond with phrases such as: "Oh, whatever you would like," or "It's doesn't matter to me, whatever the group wants to do," or

"I don't really care—whatever makes you happy." The passive person will do whatever they can to avoid telling the truth about what they want.

When it comes to intimately communicating, verbally or otherwise, the passive person will avoid this type of personal interaction. They won't truly tell you how they feel or what they want. They won't let someone else truly know them. You may think that you know them, but you don't. You know only the part of them that they think you want to know, the part that will create a sense of harmony.

The consequence of being passive is that the individual feels emotionally hurt. They feel this way because they are always repressing their true self. They have their real self locked up in a psychological box. They're hurting because the real self wants out of the closet so they can psychologically breathe.

The passive person is also hurting because they are always denying want they really want in their life. In any interaction within their personal life, they end up on the short end of the stick. They always lose in any conflict situation, but they lose because of their own doing.

Another emotional consequence of passive behavior is that the individual lives in a constant state of anxiety. The anxiety level varies depending with whom they are interacting, but anxiety is always present. The passive individual experiences varying degrees of anxiety, because they are always acting when they are around other people. They are always apprehensive about how their performance is coming across to other people. It's as if they are on stage in a theatrical performance, and the play that they are involved in is their life.

The conflict or tension between the passive individual's true self and the public self is what people commonly call stress. To alleviate tension, passive individuals find all kinds of ways to numb their anxiety. Probably the number one method to alleviate tension in our society is to use alcohol, good old "liquid courage." Alcohol works for a period of time, but tension comes right back once the booze wears off. There are many other methods of self-medicating besides alcohol. Drugs such as marijuana and prescription drugs are also very popular.

Sometimes a passive individual uses other ways to avoid anxiety, such as always staying busy, working out a lot in the gym, cleaning the house, running around with children, or working on the house. The last thing a passive individual wants to do is relax and just "chill out," because if they do, they will experience anxiety. Sometimes anxiety related to their split self comes out in the form of anxiety attacks.

The last characteristic of a passive person is that they avoid making choices when interacting with other people. They will just go with the flow of the group or within a relationship. Making any kind of choice risks the possibility of conflict and this is something they want to avoid at all costs. After years of avoiding making choices in their personal life, the passive person doesn't really know what their desires or preferences might be even if they wanted to make a choice. Over time, they gradually lose sight of who they really are.

Not only do they not know what they want in their life from minor to major choices, but they also don't know what they need to feel fulfilled in their lives. They have been so busy attentively focusing on the needs of those around them that they have forgotten their own emotional needs. When a person's emotional needs are not attended to, they will develop both physical and psychological symptoms.

When a person's needs aren't fulfilled, they experience a great deal of psychological pain, and then the pain turns to anger. The passive person experiences these emotions on an unconscious level, because if you ask them directly if they are experiencing these feelings they will say of course not, and deny that they are unhappy. They can't let their emotional truth be known to others and themselves.

The symptoms are there for others to see— such as depression, overeating, or alcohol abuse; but if you ask the passive person why they have these issues, they will not know. They don't know, because they are unwilling to admit to anything real on an emotional level.

Being Involved in a Relationship with a Passive Person

When I ask my college students what's it like dating a passive person or living with them in a committed relationship, they respond they find the other person boring, or it's frustrating, aggravating, and lonely. You would think that it would be nice and peaceful living with a passive person, but it's not. It might be that way at first, but after a while, it gets pretty old. It's like living with a clone of you, and that can get tedious.

Emotionally, when you are involved with a passive person, you feel guilty and angry. You feel guilty because after a while, you realize that you are getting everything you want, which is an enjoyable experience at first, but you soon find that it's coming at your partners' emotional expense, and they aren't getting anything they want. With this realization, the guilt starts to kick in, and the enjoyment of getting everything you want is tainted.

The other emotional reaction to being involved with a passive person is anger and frustration. The anger comes because all the responsibility for any decision is deferred to the passive person's partner. The passive person wants no part of any conflict resolution process, so they default all the decision making to their partner—from where to go to dinner to whether to buy a house. It's easy at first to have all the decision-making power, with no one to argue with your choice—whatever you want, you get. However, after a period of time all this responsibility becomes aggravating, and it starts to create resentment and anger towards the passive partner for their lack of participation. It's also irritating that if the decision made is incorrect, the blame never falls on the passive partner.

Because the passive person never states what they want or participates in any decision-making within a relationship, they seem like the ideal person to have as a partner. After a while, however, this easy, nice, go-with- the flow style starts to wear thin. The labels for the passive person go from positive sounding to more derogatory: milquetoast, doormat, pushover—and if it's a male who is the passive person, the question of "who wears the pants in the family" may start being used.

What happens is the passive individual is losing the respect of their partner. At first, they were almost idolized for being such a nice person, but now they are treated with disdain. When you are involved with a passive partner, you may like getting your way, but at the same time, you don't respect them for not taking care of themselves by communicating their desires or by establishing boundaries within the relationship.

One common example of this dynamic is the husband who has a passive wife at home in the suburbs, someone who has given up her sense of self to play the role of being the supporting, doting, good wife and mother, and he is involved in an extramarital affair. He doesn't respect his wife, but he enjoys the support and services she provides. At another level, he holds her in a certain amount of contempt and is emotionally bored in their relationship. Because his wife seems to love him unconditionally, which gives him a childlike sense of security, he may seek out a relationship with a woman who is a professional, working and living in the city. She is the total opposite of his wife because she presents a challenge to him in many ways, and this excites him. She is very passionate and emotionally present, which gives him that sense of intense involvement. At the same time, he wouldn't consider living with her, because she would be too threatening to his need for emotional security. His life becomes compartmentalized into the world of the city, with the woman he is having an affair with, and his life with his wife and kids in the suburbs. This same scenario can happen with a passive husband and a wife who has an affair with a man who is the opposite of her husband. The man she gets involved with can be someone at work or a neighbor down the street—all that is needed is accessibility and a lack of respect for her spouse.

When you are involved with a passive person, you are always getting what you want, and at first, this just seems wonderful. This sense of compatibility can be incredibly seductive when you first start getting involved in a new relationship and even into marriage. The absence of any conflict is seen as a virtue and a positive indication that the couple is meant to be together.

When I hear that there is no conflict in the relationship, I immediately become suspicious that I am not hearing the truth, and that what is occurring is a false sense of harmony, which is the goal of the passive individual. The emotional cost of this false harmony is that the passive person is developing a great sense of resentment as they adapt and lose themselves to avoid any possible conflict.

This pattern in which the passive person builds up this resentment over time is what I call the "pay later plan." The timeframe for later depends on the relationship and the individuals involved, but at some point, payment will be made. When an individual is involved with a passive person, they will pay because of all the resentments their passive partner has been repressing and storing finally come to the surface in many destructive ways. They have collected all this "debt" from their partner, and they want to be paid back. Of course, their partner didn't have a clue that this resentment existed, or didn't want to know, so they never scratched the veneer of the false harmony that existed within their relationship. All they know is that they carried on getting what they wanted and didn't realize that there was an emotional cost in the form of their partner's resentment.

I had a personal experience of this when I was single and learned the pay later plan the hard way. I was dating a woman named Karen who seemed like the perfect person for me at the time. Karen loved to do all the things that I was passionate about at that time. She loved the same music and liked going to see my favorite groups in concert; she liked the same movies, the same restaurants, and the same sports that I was crazy about—tennis and skiing. She also liked all my friends and wanted to socialize with them. I thought I was in relationship heaven. Jane seemed too good to be true. (Therein lies one big red flag.)

Our compatibility continued for at least a month until one day she said, "Dan, I want to spend next weekend with my parents at their cabin in the mountains. Does that sound like something you would like to do?" I replied, "I don't think so. I'm not really ready to meet your parents quite yet, maybe in another month or so." Karen's reaction totally shocked me. She said, "You don't want to go visit my parents now? This is something that I want to do with you. I can't believe that you won't do this for me after all that I have been doing for you." I responded with, "What do you mean 'after all you have been doing for me?'" She said, "Like those stupid concerts. I hate the music you like, and those dumb movies are so boring, and your crazy friends that I had to endure." My comeback was, "Wait a minute, Karen, I thought you did all those things because you wanted to and that you enjoyed your experience." Karen said, "Dan, I did all of those things just to make you happy. I didn't really want to do them, and now I can't believe that you won't see my parents." In her mind, it was time to be paid back for her selling out herself and being passive in the moment. It was time for me to pay.

Often the passive partner can flip and take all their built-up resentment and become the aggressive partner in an attempt to compensate for all the time that they were passive within the relationship. Unfortunately, this approach doesn't work at creating an atmosphere of love and intimacy between the couple. It's just trading one ineffective behavior pattern for another.

THE CONSEQUENCES OF PASSIVE BEHAVIOR

One of the biggest consequences of acting in a passive manner within the context of a person's personal life—as opposed to their business or corporate world—is that they are unable to experience any true intimacy with others. Because they can't truly communicate what's really true in terms of their emotions or desires, no one knows them intimately. They only let others know them on a very superficial level, which can leave them feeling lonely, isolated, and hurting for some real connection to another person.

Can you trust the passive individual? They are really nice and easy to get along with in a relationship. They never argue or fight with you. The answer is a resounding no. You can't trust a passive person because you never know what's true or real about them. They are like Karen—you think everything is compatible on the surface, but it's all fake. What's really going on is impossible to know.

The passive person is unable to truly communicate within a relationship. I have taught many passive clients how to communicate in an effective manner. They have the knowledge to communicate well, but because of their passivity, they still are inhibited from communicating what's true for them. They won't allow themselves to take any personal risk, because they are afraid of what might happen if they spoke the truth.

Because a passive person doesn't allow their true self to come through, they never allow anyone to really know them. Because of their inhibition, the passive individual is unable to receive any real validation from others, and they end up having low self-esteem as a result. The validation they do receive is more about their act, because their true self is not exposed to receive any positive recognition.

Their low self-esteem reinforces their need to act in a passive way. Their thinking is, "If I don't act this way, no one will want to be involved with me." The more they act in a passive manner, the lower their self-esteem goes, so it all becomes a spiraling down pattern that drives their self-esteem into oblivion.

The last major consequence of acting in a passive manner in an individual's personal life is the buildup of a great deal of resentment and anger. The resentment develops because passive people don't allow themselves to express their true self. They keep it hidden; it's as if they locked themselves up in their own psychological prison. As the Eagles said in their song, "Hotel California," "We are all just prisoners here, of our own device." This is how I view passive people. The good news is that passive people hold the key to their own freedom.

Living your life in a psychological prison is toxic to an individual's mental and physical health. The anger at being locked up and inhibited is repressed. Over time, this repressed anger and resentment turns into depression in various degrees. As time goes, on the level of resentment increases and the individual has to use more and more of their energy to hold the resentment back from being expressed. This energy drain wears a person out, especially if there are other areas in their life that also are draining their energy resources such as a job or children. Without much energy, the passive-acting person doesn't have much passion to partake in the pleasures of their life, such as sex, sports, or just participating with their family. They are just tired all the time and want to sleep.

The passive person lives their life in a constant state of conflict between their true self that wants to break out of the psychological prison and the scared self that acts as the jailer, which creates a great deal of emotional anxiety and tension. The common label of this condition is what people call stress.

The more an individual is in a state of constant stress—whether consciously or not—the more the tension takes a toll on the individual immune system by lowering the body's ability to fight off diseases. The passive individual is opening the door to all kinds of medical problems that will play a role in shorting their life span.

AGGRESSIVE BEHAVIOR

The other option of behavior in our culture is known as being aggressive. Traditionally, men have been more aggressive in their behavior, but as our culture has changed and become more androgynous, many women have adopted the aggressive style as well. Being aggressive became necessary for women who entered the work force and participated in highly competitive situations within the corporate world. As with the passive style of behavior, aggressive behavior has no place within the context of an intimate relationship, regardless of gender.

Popular labels for someone who acts in an aggressive manner are tough, strong, pushy, abrupt, bully, or inconsiderate. A woman who acts in aggressive manner may be labeled with these adjectives, but in addition, she might be called a bitch, ball-buster, or butch, because of her gender. Some of these labels could be viewed as positive, depending on the circumstances, but using these labels is destructive in creating a safe place for intimacy to develop.

Characteristics of an Aggressive Individual

I am going to discuss the impact of aggressive behavior within the context of a committed intimate relationship. When someone acts in an aggressive manner, their intent is to make things better for themselves, but they will act this way no matter how it might affect their partner. They will get what they want or need no matter how their partner feels. To an aggressive person, emotions have no real meaning in any conflict situation.

Another characteristic of someone who is acting in an aggressive manner is that they have no inhibitions in the way they communicate. Their manner of speech is no-holds-barred. They will tell you their opinions, desires or emotions, whether you want to hear them or not. They are "in your face" with their communication.

The problem with the aggressive communication style is that it comes across as very condescending. Aggressive people communicate with a critical parent approach. They don't ask if you want to hear what they have to say or ask you if this is a good time to talk. Instead, they just barge into your personal space without respecting any of your boundaries, and tell you what you should or should not do and why. Did you ask for their input? You probably didn't, but they just tell you anyway.

Not only is the aggressive approach of communication condescending, but it's also usually delivered in the form of criticism or a personal put-down. A partner who has an aggressive style of behavior will not be supportive of your self-esteem. In fact, over time they will tear your self-worth down. They are truly toxic within the context of an intimate relationship.

The next characteristic of someone who acts in an aggressive manner is that they take control of conflict situations. Their way takes precedence over their partner: it's "their way or the highway." The aggressive partner is the boss, the dictator, the head of the house. [Stereotypically, the man takes on the aggressive approach in a relationship, but women often take this role as well, and a major role reversal occurs. Regardless of who acts in an aggressive manner, it's destructive to an intimate relationship.

There is no decision-making process when an aggressive-acting person is involved in some type of conflict. The attitude of sitting down and talking about the conflict and figuring out how it can be resolved amicably does not come into play. The aggressive-acting partner makes the decision for you, so in their mind, the conflict is resolved. For example, they tell you where you are going to go on a vacation, or where you are going to dinner, or what movie you are going to watch.

The bottom line with an aggressive partner is that they are going to win and get their way no matter what you do or say. They will dominate the situation even if you end up emotionally hurt by the situation. You will lose and be unhappy about the situation and the relationship.

Being Involved with an Aggressive Partner

When a person lives with an aggressive person, one thing is clear: you don't get what you want. As I like to say, "Just forget about it." You are coming out on the losing end, which isn't going to create an atmosphere of intimacy on any level. After a while, you start to forget about the things you like. It becomes easier to just lose yourself instead of engaging in the constant fight and struggle with the aggressive partner's approach to the relationship. The loss of your self-identity can have devastating psychological consequences in the long run.

When you are involved with an aggressive partner, they attacking, judge, and criticize you whenever they can, so this constantly puts you on the defensive. You never know when they are going take a verbal shot, so your guard has to be up all the time. This is a very stressful way to live, because of all the anxiety you experience by "walking on egg shells" and never knowing when your partner will explode with their toxic communication.

The aggressive individual will also try to shame and humiliate you when they can. They want you to feel terrible about yourself, with a secret mission to destroy your self-esteem. It can be very unnerving to go to any social function with an aggressive partner, especially if they consume alcohol, because this is an atmosphere where they can do the most damage. As a couple, you are around other people and friends, so you can be a sitting duck for the kind of humiliation and embarrassment the aggressive partner can inflict.

The ultimate consequence of having a relationship with an aggressive person is that you will end up feeling a great deal of hurt, anger, and frustration. You will be unable to communicate these emotions to your aggressive partner, because they aren't interested in your emotions, so opening yourself up and sharing how you feel is just inviting more pain and disappointment into your life. These emotions become internalized and "stuffed," or repressed, over time.

You experience the hurt and anger because your entire being is put on hold. There is no real self-expression or communication of any desires or wants. In any conflict situation, you lose. You are being verbally abused and dismissed, all of which is going to feel emotionally hurtful and make you resentful.

The repressed anger gets expressed in many ways, but is generally not released in any constructive or healthy manner. Repressed anger often manifests in the form of depression to various degrees. Sometimes the repressed hurt and anger are expressed physically, with psychosomatic reactions such as headaches, anxiety attacks, and stomach difficulties.

The repressed hurt and anger can be expressed through what is called acting-out behavior, like having extramarital affairs, shoplifting, and alcohol or drug abuse. In some cases, the passive partner explodes with their stuffed anger and then they start acting in an aggressive manner in the relationship. It's as if they have so much anger that they can't take it anymore, and "come out with guns blazing." There is a role reversal in the power and control aspect of their relationship.

The Consequences for a Person Who Acts in an Aggressive Manner

Within the context of an intimate relationship, acting in an aggressive manner has only negative outcomes over a period of time. The first result is that the individual who behaves aggressively won't experience a great deal of intimacy with their partner. Their partner will build a psychological wall between them to create an emotional distance as a form of defense. It's difficult to be close and intimate with a separating wall. Who would want to be intimate with an aggressive person who doesn't care how you feel, who only wants their desires fulfilled, and has no respect for your personal boundaries? Not anyone who loves himself.

The second consequence for someone who acts in an aggressive manner is that their self-esteem is going to be lowered or destroyed, assuming they had any in the first place. One of the confusing aspects of aggressive behavior is that people who act this way present themselves as exuding high self-esteem and confidence. They have a certain bravado about themselves that makes their partner believe they are self-assured, but in reality, they have really low self-esteem, and they present themselves this way to compensate for their insecurity. They don't believe in themselves, so they have to hype the "product." It's as they're a salesperson trying to sell something they don't really believe has worth. They have to tell you how great and fantastic they are and why you are lucky to have them in your life. It's over the top, which in turn makes them come on even stronger. Their partner finally caves in and says, "Fine, you made the sale," but deep down you don't really believe anything the aggressive person is telling you, because their words and the way they act don't coincide.

How could someone who acts aggressively have any self-esteem? They are inconsiderate, insensitive, and dismissive of the emotions of those who are close to them. They are not going to receive a whole lot of positive validation from their partner for the way they act. The aggressive partner knows they are alienating those close to them; however, they can't admit this fact, so they pretend how great they are, but they know that behind their bravado they don't really like themselves.

The ultimate consequence for the aggressive person is that their partner will leave them. The fear of abandonment is what drives their aggressive behavior and paradoxically creates the very scenario they don't want to happen: that their partner leaves the relationship.

The most common example of where aggressive behavior creates eventual abandonment is when one or both partners say they have a jealousy problem. The partner who is jealous usually acts in an aggressive manner in the relationship. They try to control their partner on any level within the relationship that they find threatening to their security. They start telling their partner what they can wear, who they can talk to or have lunch with, or who they can dance with at their friends' wedding. These are usually demands, not requests, and they don't care if their partner is comfortable with these limitations. It's all about "medicating" their fear of abandonment by controlling their partner's actions.

This attempted control has nothing to do with love or romance. Don't confuse the need for control as a loving gesture, because it's not. It's totally inappropriate between two adults. The need for control may start out on a minor level, but over time, the need to control escalates because the fear isn't resolved. The jealous partner never really trusts that their partner is with them as a choice, but rather because they think they have control over their partner.

Not too many adults want to be controlled by another adult. They resent that they are being told what they can and can't do, and this repressed resentment and anger will create a great deal of emotional distance between them and their jealous, aggressive partner. This distance creates even more anxiety for the jealous partner, so they try to control their partner even more. The cycle just keeps increasing until finally the partner who is being controlled says they've had enough, and leaves the relationship.

The Assertive Style of Behavior: The Choice that Works in Intimate, Committed Relationships

Now that I have discussed the passive and aggressive behavior choices that our culture offers and the effect they have on our personal relationships and our self-esteem, I want to talk about a third option. As I mentioned in the beginning of this chapter, that option is being assertive.

What is it like to act assertively? Assertive behavior often gets confused with being aggressive, but there are some critical differences.

When a person is acting in an assertive manner, they are trying to take care of themselves in terms of their desires. They are taking care of themselves, but not trying to do so at the emotional expense of their partner. They care about how their partner feels, unlike someone who acts aggressively. The aggressive person is trying to dominate their partner, but at the same time, they won't give themselves up by repressing the communication of their wants like a passive person.

Another aspect of an assertive person is that they tell you what they want. There is no confusion about their desire. They tell you what their choice is without deferring the decision back to you like a passive person does when asked.

An assertive person doesn't tell you what your choice or desire should be by devaluing your choice, which is characteristic of an aggressive person. The assertive person gives you the opportunity to express your own desire if you so choose.

When an assertive person states their desire, they are psychologically taking care of themselves. They are stating their own boundaries regarding what does or does not work for them. When you act in an assertive manner, your self-esteem is going to increase. With more self-esteem, it is easier to assert yourself. So assertiveness and self-esteem feed off each other in a positive way. In contrast, passive and aggressive behaviors destroy an individual's self-esteem.

When an assertive individual expresses their desires, they do so with the expectation that they may or may not get what they want. They don't demand that every desire they have be fulfilled to its utmost. This expectation is the major difference between aggressive and assertive behaviors. The aggressive individual expects to get everything they want and will fight and push until they get it fulfilled. Often when someone becomes assertive in their life, people close to them immediately think that when they express a desire they are being selfish and aggressive, when in fact they are just stating that they want something. Rather than demanding that their desire be fulfilled, they are putting it out there to start a negotiation process to see how their wants might be fulfilled. When you want to change from being passive or aggressive to becoming assertive, it's important to tell your partner that you are making this change and that your expectation is to be informative as opposed to demanding. This way, they will have a better sense of where you are coming from when you state a desire or want and are less likely to be threatened or defensive.

When a person acts in an assertive manner within a relationship, it gives their partner the opportunity to be assertive as well. When the assertive person expresses their want, they are in a sense inviting their partner to do the same. Just because the assertive partner gives their partner the opportunity to be assertive doesn't automatically mean they will do so.

An assertive partner generally threatens a passive person. They feel threatened, because they are being encouraged to disclose their truth, which for a passive person is very unsettling. When a passive individual is involved with an assertive partner, it becomes obvious that they are not expressing their wants; generally, an assertive person isn't going to be comfortable with that behavior and will confront the passive person about it.

An aggressive person is going to be upset and frustrated with an assertive partner. The assertive partner won't allow the aggressive-acting partner to dominate and control them and the relationship. The assertive partner sets boundaries and sticks to them, which drives the aggressive partner crazy, because all their attempts to control and dominate have no effect. The assertive partner doesn't cave in and give their power away.

THE COMMUNICATIVE STYLES OF PASSIVE, AGGRESSIVE, AND ASSERTIVE BEHAVIORS

Each of the three behavior styles has its own characteristic communication approach. The passive person's form of communication is basically no real communication, besides "I don't care." You ask them where they want to go to dinner and they will respond, "I don't care" or "whatever, it doesn't matter," or "whatever you would like." None of these responses gives you the sense of knowing what they are really thinking.

Someday I might open a chain of restaurants called the "I Don't Care Restaurant." It sells all types of fast food like hamburgers, pizza, tacos, and so on. It will have it all, so when I ask my kids where they want to go for lunch and they tell me "I don't care," I will know the exact place, right out there on the Interstate, the I Don't Care Restaurant.

The aggressive individual's communicative approach is to use what are called "You messages." These messages are very critical and condescending and put the receiver on the defensive. They are very parental in nature, and that's why an aggressive person likes them, because it gives them the sense that they are in control. These are some examples of "You messages": "You don't do anything right around here," "You need to work out in the gym, because you need to lose some weight," or "You are just too emotional."

The assertive individual's communicative approach is to use what are typically called "I messages." These statements clearly define the speaker's desires or wants. When an assertive person is asked what they want for dinner they will tell you, "I want Chinese food." You will know their truth, without being attacked and without them demanding that what they want must be satisfied. They are just putting their desire on the table to start a negotiation if necessary.

What is a Passive-Aggressive Person?

Many people use the passive-aggressive label within relationships, but I am not sure they always know what it really means. It seems straightforward: a person who is passive and aggressive acts both ways. This is true in a way, but the aggressive behavior that is expressed comes across in a passive way.

When a passive-aggressive person is faced with a conflict situation within a relationship, their first choice of action is to be passive and adapt to avoid the conflict and immediately create a sense of harmony. Their partner believes that the conflict has been resolved, and that what they want is going to be fulfilled. As time goes by, they realize that what they thought was going to occur isn't happening, and they ask their passive-aggressive partner what's going on. Their partner reassures them that they will do what they agreed to do, but they don't. They just "blow off" their agreement with their partner with an indifference to their partner's emotions, and this is the aggressive aspect of this behavior style.

Having been a passive-aggressive teenager, I can give an example that frequently occurred at that time in my home. Every Saturday morning, my mother would expect me to cut our lawn. I was the designated gardener in our family. She would say, "Dan, I want you to get the lawn mowed by 9 am." I would respond, "Sure, Mom, I will be right out there and cut the grass." If the truth were told, I had no desire to cut the lawn, but I told her I would do it. An hour or two later, she realized that the grass still wasn't cut, and I was watching television.

Now with a raised voice, she would say, "Dan, get out there and cut the grass like you said you would!"

"Oh, I am sorry, Mom, I will get right on it."

"OK, I am going to the store, and when I get back I expect the grass to be cut."

"Ok, Mom, see you later," I said.

She came back from the store and saw that I hadn't done what I said I would do. At this point, she became enraged, and yelled, "You get your ass out there right this minute, and I going to watch until you get that mower going and I see that you are doing what you said."

"Ok, Mom, I am sorry, I just forgot."

She responded, "Yeah, right, you forgot, or you just don't want to mow the lawn. Give me a break."

This is an example of a passive-aggressive power struggle. I couldn't come out and tell her, "Forget about me mowing the lawn. I am not your gardener. If you want your damn lawn mowed, hire a real gardener because I have better things to do on a Saturday." This type of honest expression wouldn't have gone over well with her, and most likely, I would be punished in some manner. She was the boss, and I had no choice. We weren't in an equal adult relationship, so I dealt with her authority by being passive-aggressive, and hoped that she would forget and I wouldn't have to cut the lawn. Unfortunately, this approach never worked out for me. The major consequence is that a passive-aggressive person loses all credibility with people that they interact with in their everyday life. No one trusts them, because they just don't do what they say.

The example I gave was between a parent and child, but the same pattern occurs between adults. People who manage office buildings can be good at being passive-aggressive, because they tell you what you want to hear up front. For example, they will assure you that "Yes, I will have an air-conditioning repair person out there today," and then they don't show for another couple days. In the meantime, you're sweating in a heat wave in an office that doesn't have windows that open.

What Are the Beliefs that Drive Someone to Act in a Passive or Aggressive Manner?

If you want to change from being aggressive or passive, it's important to understand the cognitive beliefs that play a role influencing these two behavior choices. An aggressive person has very low self-esteem, even though they won't let you know this fact. They believe they aren't lovable as they are because of their low self-esteem in relation to being a loving partner. Because of this insecurity and its accompanying fear of abandonment, an aggressive person compensates by acting in an overtly controlling, dominating manner. Their control increases and intensifies in response to any behaviors of their partner that they deem threatening to their emotional or financial security.

A passive person has the same belief as an aggressive individual, which is that they are not lovable as they are, so the only way to get someone to be with them is to compensate by trying to control the relationship. The difference between an aggressive and a passive person is that the passive partner controls things covertly. It isn't obvious on the surface of interacting with them that controlling behavior is occurring, whereas it's clear that an aggressive partner is trying to control the relationship.

Passive individuals sometimes become upset when I tell them that they are acting in a controlling, manipulative manner. They take offense at the label because they see themselves, as nice people, and being controlling and manipulative are what mean people do in their relationships.

The passive partner manipulates and controls the relationship by censoring the truth. They present a false self, so there is no real conflict within the relationship to fabricate a false sense of harmony.

The core belief that both passive and aggressive people psychologically operate from is that they don't believe they are lovable as they are, which requires that they become controlling. This need for control destroys any intimate relationship in the end. When control is operating in a personal relationship, the intimacy is lost, and the anger and resentment that is repressed builds, which further distances a couple. It's sad that the two major behavior style options modeled for us in our culture—passive and aggressive—create nothing but dysfunctional intimate relationships.

It's no wonder that so many couples have difficulty maintaining any intimacy in their marriages. The only behavior style that contributes to maintaining intimacy in a committed relationship is being assertive.

I don't want you to think that there isn't a time and place for passive or aggressive behavior, because there are circumstances when either behavior style is appropriate. For instance, in any competitive situation, whether it's in business or on the playing field, it makes sense to be aggressive. When I go out and play competitive tennis, I am out there to win, not lose. I am not too concerned about how my opponent feels about losing the match. I am sure that lawyers feel the same way when they win a case in court.

It's also appropriate to be passive at times. You need to learn this style of behavior if you want to be political within the corporate world. I am not suggesting that you want to be passive all the time, but at certain times, like when you are interacting with a supervisor or the CEO of the corporation, it may be suitable. They are paying you to be passive to some degree, and the pay-off is financial security. I learned to be passive when my mother-in-law would come for a weekend visit. I wanted to present a false sense of harmony, because anything else wouldn't be worth the conflict. Being intimate or telling the truth wouldn't work. I just wanted to get along for that short period of time, and it made my wife happy, which always brought me dividends.

If You Act in Either a Passive or Aggressive Way Is It Possible to Change?

Can a person who acts in an aggressive or passive manner develop assertive behavior in their personal life? The answer is a resounding yes. Aggressive and passive behaviors are learned and driven by a basic fear of abandonment within the context of an individual's personal life. An individual can be aggressive or assertive when they go to work, for example, but at the end of the day when they come home to be with their spouse, they may act in a passive manner. Different psychological factors occur outside of a personal relationship that can influence the way that someone acts, but in personal relationships, it's usually the fear of abandonment that is the key to changing a person's behavioral style. Personality types and biological factors such as hormones can influence behavioral styles, but we have cognitive reasoning that can overrule biology.

If a person has the ability to change their behavioral style, the next question is what motivates them to make this change in the first place? Ideally, their motivation would be the realization that acting passively or aggressively prevents them from developing an emotionally intimate relationship, and the desire for emotional intimacy is something that they might want to experience in their personal life. Another positive motivation would be that they want to have better self-esteem and be able to love themselves. These are all positive cognitive reasons that you think would be enough to make the change, but from my experience, logical reasons usually don't motivate someone to change their behavior.

In my teens and up to my mid-twenties, I was really passive when it came to my personal relationships with women. Not many people believe that who know me today, but I was passive back then, and I made the change to becoming assertive later. People often ask how I made this transformation in behavioral style. I believe that there wasn't just one factor that played a role in influencing my personal liberation.

The first component that played a role was the emotional anxiety. Being passive with the women I would date and have a relationship with caused me a great deal of anxiety. I was a nervous wreck dating women, especially someone who I really liked right away. The more I was attracted, the more anxiety I experienced. This anxious reaction started in high school, continued through college, and into my twenties. I would try to self-medicate the anxiety with alcohol, but that would only make the situation worse, because I worried about being too intoxicated and being more foolish. When I was twenty-six, I was a full-time practicing therapist and was very aware of my emotions, and I just couldn't take experiencing all this anxiety and stress in my relationships with women.

I wanted to stop being passive, and to be real in my personal life as soon as possible. I no longer wanted to "act" in my personal life with women. If they didn't like the real me, then I would rather be alone. When I stopped acting, I relaxed and the tension between the fake and the real me went away, and I didn't need any artificial substances to accomplish this state of being.

When I stopped acting and shared my true self with the woman I was dating, I took a psychological risk. The risk I was taking was that I might be rejected, with the result of being alone. But I decided I would rather be alone on a Saturday night than face being in a relationship where I was stressed-out and full of anxiety, and where I was constantly trying to please my date, regardless of how I felt. Being passive in my personal life didn't sound like fun anymore.

The other emotional factor that contributed to motivating me to act in an assertive manner with women was that I got over my fear of abandonment. I started to realize that when I relaxed with the woman I was dating, as opposed to being a nervous wreck, I became more attractive. What a shock—they liked me, and I was not acting. That's not to say that they all liked my true self, but I only needed a few girlfriends. All this was the result of taking the risk of showing my true self and not some fabricated identity based on what I thought the woman wanted in a man. I soon realized that there are lots of women in the world I could choose to be with. In my passive days, I always thought that every relationship was my last chance to make it work or I would fall into the abyss of loneliness. With this newfound confidence, I was able to be assertive in my relationships with women and could ask myself the question, "Do I need to be with her or do I want to be with her?" The answer was I no longer needed to be with a woman. I had recovered from my emotional dependency and it changed the way I interacted with women in my personal life.

Aggressive people can change when they realize the psychological "price tag" for their behavior choice. They have to hit bottom and start looking inward and stop blaming others for their behavior. They need to be willing to look at their need to control others, and what it means not to have control. Once the aggressive person addresses their control issues, they need to learn what it means to be assertive.

The aggressive person can't just drop being aggressive. They need to understand an alternative behavior style that isn't passive. Many times people are aggressive, because their fear is that they will be dominated and become passive.

It's not uncommon for passive people who want to make a change to become assertive to start acting in an aggressive manner first. They generally have so much built-up anger that it comes out as aggressiveness to make up for all the time they had been letting people walk all over them. When they realize this approach isn't working, they finally learn to become assertive.

Chapter Eleven

The Conclusion: Bringing It All Together

N ow that you have reached the end of this book, I hope that your awareness of what it means to love yourself has been increased. I hope that you have a greater understanding of what the phrase, "you have to love yourself before you can love somebody else," really means.

Now that you have a greater awareness about how to love yourself, the challenge is how to take what you have learned from this book and apply it to your daily life. Go out there and make it real. Don't let this just be another self-help book that you have read and then let all the information you learned sit on the shelf.

I want to review the two key components covered earlier that influence personal growth and change. The first component is the issue of motivation. I can teach people all kinds of ways to make their life better, but are they motivated to make the changes required? As I stated earlier in the book, it all comes down to emotions. Are you hurt, angry, or frustrated enough to make the changes? Another powerful motivating emotion is fear. The fear of the consequences puts the fire under our rear ends to leave our comfort zones. The fear of getting type 2 diabetes recently motivated me to change my diet. Fear can also act to inhibit change, if there is more fear than emotional discomfort. Pay attention to your emotions; they provide the needed fuel that enables you to "walk the talk."

The last component that's key to making changes in your life is to create an atmosphere of acceptance, as opposed to one that's judgmental. Don't involve yourself with people who are critical, judgmental, and generally no fun to be around. These psychologically toxic individuals will only inhibit you from taking any risks and making positive changes so that you will be able to grow and thrive in your life.

As important as it is to stay away from toxic people, it's also important to get rid of the critical judgmental part of your own psyche. This part of your psychological makeup's intention is to keep you from taking any risks and moving out of your comfort zone. I don't think you can totally get rid of this critical part completely, but at least you can redirect your self-comments to be more loving and, above all, self-accepting.

LOVE YOURSELF
Daniel Beaver
July 25, 2010

BIBLIOGRAPHY

Alberti, Robert, and Emmons, Michael. *Your Perfect Right: A Guide to Assertive Behavior.* San Luis Obispo, CA: Impact Publishers, 1970.

Bach, George, and Goldberg, Herb. *Creative Aggression.* Garden City, NY: Doubleday & Co., 1974.

Bandler, Richard; Grinder, John; Satir, Virginia. *Changing with Families.* Palo Alto, CA: Science and Behavior Books, Inc., 1976.

Beaver, Daniel, M.S. *Beyond the Marriage Fantasy, How to Create True Marital Intimacy.* San Francisco, CA: Harper& Row Publishers, 1983.

Beaver, Daniel, M.S. *More than Just Sex, A Committed Couple's Guide to Keeping Relationships Lively, Intimate & Gratifying.* Fairfield, CT: Aslan Publishers, 1991.

Beattie, Melody. *Codependent No More: How to Stop Controlling Others and Start Caring For Yourself.* City Center, MN: Hazelden, 1987.

Burns, D. David. *Feeling Good: The Mood Therapy Revised and Updated.* New York: Avon Books, 1992.

Carnes, Patrick, Ph.D. *Don't Call It Love, Recovery from Sexual Addiction.* New York: Bantam Books, 1991.

Carnes, Patrick, Ph.D. *Contrary to Love, Helping the Sexual Addict.* City Center, MN: Hazelden, 1989.

Goldberg, Herb. *Hazards of Being Male.* New York: Signet, 1976.

Halpern, M. Howard, Ph.D. *How to Break Your Addiction to a Person.* McGraw-Hill, 1982.

James, Muriel, and Jongeward, Dorothy. *Born to Win: Transactional Analysis with Gestalt Experiements.* Reading, MA: Addison-Wesley, 1971.

Jourand, Sidney. *Transparent Self.* New York: D. Van Nostrand Co., 1971.

McKay, Matthew, Ph.D., and Fanning, Patrick. *Self-Esteem.* Oakland, CA: New Harbinger Publications, 2000.

Peele, Stanton. *Love and Addiction*. New York: Taplinger Co., 1975.

Paul, Jordan, Ph.D., and Paul, Margaret, Ph.D.*Do I Have to Give Up Me to Be Loved by You*. CompCare Publishers. 1983.

Satir, Virgina. *Peoplemaking*. Palo Alto, CA: Science and Behavior Books Inc., 1972.

Sheehy, Gail. *Sex and the Seasoned Woman, Pursuing the Passionate Life*. New York: Random House, 2006.

Smith, J. Manuel. *When I Say No I Feel Guilty*. New York: Bantam Books, 1975.